EMOTIONAL PROCESSING

How to Work Your Way through Almost Anything

ALSO BY STORMY SMOLENY PH.D.

In Search of the Unwanted Self

*Truths from the Self: Insights into Finding Wisdom
in the Present Moment*

EMOTIONAL PROCESSING

How to Work Your Way through Almost Anything

Stormy Smoleny Ph.D.

Indigo Reef Publishing

Printed in the United States of America
Indigo Reef Publishing, Inc.
9150 S.W. 87th Avenue, Suite 106
Miami, FL   33176
www.indigoreefpublishing.com

First Printing: 2018
ISBN-10: 0-9789957-4-0
ISBN-13: 978-0-9789957-4-4
Library of Congress Control Number: 2017903475

Editing: Richard Firsten
Design: Integrative Ink

Quantity discounts are available on bulk purchases of this book for reselling, educational purposes, subscription incentives, corporate gifts, and fund raising. Please call Indigo Reef Publishing, Inc. at 305-253-1107 for discount rates.

Visit www.stormysmoleny.com for more information about the author and the principles set forth in *Emotional Processing*.

For Kaitlyn Wienczkowski,
my second granddaughter.

TABLE OF CONTENTS

ACKNOWLEDGMENTS

I gratefully acknowledge the contributions of my editor, Richard Firsten (RFirsten@aol.com). He is not only a superlative linguist, teacher, and author, but is as patient and insightful as any editor could be. Beyond that, he is very sensitive to allowing an author his or her own voice, always guiding and never overriding.

I also wish to acknowledge Stephanee Killen of Integrative Ink (integrativeink.com) for a beautiful cover design and interior layout. She has proven to be knowledgeable, professional, and very responsive to my needs in putting this book together. I am grateful for both her kindness and her expertise.

I would especially like to thank my husband, Charles, for his patience and loving support. His encouragement and faith in me have been a blessing.

PREFACE

*Eve*ryone who knows me well is aware of my penchant for philosophy, spirituality, and quantum physics. It's true; I'm fascinated by all things transcendent, esoteric, and holistic. This interest in things beyond rational thought and beyond the bounds of the physical realm has resulted in two previous books that contain both psychological and spiritual thought. To me the two disciplines seem inextricably intertwined.

Emotional Processing is a departure from my first two books in that it is strictly psychological in nature. It is a practical guide to working through your emotions. As such, it is meant to help you work with yourself as an individual who is subject to the limitations of the physical world.

The reality is that your power on this planet is limited (you are not omnipotent), you do not have infinite awareness, understanding, and insight (you are not omniscient), and you are presently located in a specific place and time (you are not omnipresent). Furthermore, your choices are sometimes limited, you are subject to the physical laws of this planet, you have a certain genetic predisposition, and you are dealing with a physical body that is subject to illness and eventually death. You live in a four-dimensional world (height, width, depth, and time). You have to deal with separate individuals in a very complex external environment (your outer world) and with yourself as a multifaceted, complicated human being with a compendium of thoughts, feelings, memories, strivings, and biological needs (your inner world).

Given all this, in *Emotional Processing* I've tried to keep things practical, tangible, and doable.

Yet I want all who read this book to know that everyone's existence goes beyond the physical realm. While you exist on the physical realm as dense matter, you simultaneously exist on the nonphysical realm as light, movement, and energy. The latter realm is found on the subatomic level. On a subatomic level all is very different. There you have fewer limitations to your power, knowledge, and presence. You do not struggle with a physical body and its constraints. You exist as pure energy. You can move and create at will. Your power, knowledge, and presence are boundless. You do not get sick and die; you are eternal (energy cannot be destroyed; it can only change forms).

Such a realm has been discovered through quantum physics; it is definitely there. This realm and other nonphysical realms can be accessed through altered states of consciousness brought forth by meditation, receptive prayer, inner listening, mindfulness, and immersion in the present moment. There is great value in this, and it is worth your consideration. However, there is a caveat.

The subatomic realm described above is also known as the spiritual realm (spiritual meaning nonphysical, transcendent, unlimited). Many of us relate to the nonphysical realm as spiritual in nature and therefore revere it. Consequently, we largely rely on spiritual practices to solve our problems and function well. This is fine in one regard; however, it should not be the only thing we rely on. The problem is this: While we are ethereal beings on a higher level, we are also physical beings with mass and density. This fact cannot be escaped. We have difficulties here that we do not have on a higher level. Different rules apply. Higher level rules that do apply bring slower results. Some of them are completely misunderstood. In addition, we do not live in a continual state of altered consciousness. Most of us are only aware of being here on the physical plane. Consequently, we have to deal with life as human beings on planet Earth.

I would encourage you to explore all possibilities for a better life, but I would not suggest attempting to substitute spiritual practices for psychological ones. It is true that the two can overlap. You can do both, but you can't effectively substitute the spiritual for the psychological. I say this because in my spiritual pursuits I have known people who could access the higher realms regularly, but their lives were a mess. Along with their spiritual practices, they were doing all kinds of unacceptable things. They were still having affairs. They still couldn't get along with their significant others, function well at work, or understand what made them behave as they did. They still exhibited addictive behaviors, suffered from anxiety, got depressed, and lost their tempers. This is because they never mastered the physical realm.

I remember what it was like to be so familiar with the higher realms after years of spiritual practice, only to still struggle with the mundane problems of life. I had been holding myself to a lofty standard, not realizing that here on Earth I was dealing with a very different kind of situation. Specifically, I was dealing with a very limited realm and with very limited powers as a human being.

When I began to learn about myself as a human being and all the limitations it entailed, there was a profound healing. I no longer erroneously told myself that I had unlimited power and that I had simply failed to exercise it correctly. I no longer berated myself for not having known something ahead of time. I no longer deluded myself into thinking that I had unlimited choices. I no longer assumed that others behaved as they did because of something I did or did not do. I no longer told myself that every life event has a string attached leading back to me, that I was the center of the universe. I learned how to occasionally be helpless. I learned how to be imperfect. I learned how to accept the limitations of this plane of existence.

All this was a game changer. I would like to change the game for you as well.

So I offer you this practical guide to working with your emotions not as a naysayer of spiritual practice, but as an addition to it. It is not my intention to rob you of what the higher realms can offer (particularly the blessed sense of connection to the universe that it provides), but it is to help you deal more effectively with your life here and to protect you from attacking yourself for your human limitations.

Now let's get started mastering life on planet Earth.

Stormy Smoleny Ph.D.

EMOTIONAL PROCESSING

Basic Considerations

Chapter 1

KNOW YOUR GOALS

When it comes to achieving emotional balance, there is one master goal that we all need to have and upon which all other goals rely. This is the goal of knowing ourselves. Another way to say this is that we must have the goal of becoming more aware of our inner processes (thoughts, feelings, and impulses) and the behaviors they generate.

Whether we are trying to move beyond a painful feeling or an unhealthy behavior, the starting point is always the same — awareness of self. This is partially because we cannot change what we do not know exists. We cannot be less self-absorbed if we are not aware that we are self-absorbed. We cannot be less critical and demanding if we are unaware of being just that. We cannot delay our gratification and thus be more discerning in our choices if we are not aware that we are impulsively grasping at each possibility for need fulfillment as it comes along.

In a similar vein, we cannot work through painful feelings if we are unaware of exactly what they are. For instance, we may feel generally depressed yet not be aware that underneath our depression we feel angry, sad, afraid, lonely, or helpless. Or we may feel generally anxious, but be unaware that beneath this we feel angry, sad, alone, needy, or unsure. Worse yet, we may be so emotionally anesthetized that we cannot feel anything at all.

Awareness of self is the starting point not only so that we can identify what we are working with, but also have the opportunity to compassionately attend to our feelings and carefully examine the thoughts that underlie them. This is called emotional processing. It gives us a chance to minister to the emotional self until it is soothed, correct any errors in our thought processes, and arrive at a more balanced point of view. Through this process we are able to achieve emotional release and obtain a greater sense of stability.

The average person is only aware of about 12% to 15% of that which is going on within his or her psyche. That is pretty dismal in the awareness department. Such limited awareness not only leaves us awash with uncomfortable, highly-charged feelings seeking release, but also allows us very little control over our behaviors. This is the case because without constructive processing, our intense feelings break loose in an unrestrained manner, and then we are reduced to reacting rather than consciously choosing. In such a state of unconsciousness, we are pawns of whatever is swimming around in the murky depths of our unconscious; we are relegated to unrelenting states of emotional pain and a world of childish, impulsive reactivity.

It may be helpful to envision our conscious/unconscious interplay in a visual manner. First imagine a large circle which represents the sum total of all that goes on within us. This circle includes all of our thoughts, feelings, and impulses. Initially, they are all living in the darkness of unconsciousness. As such, they cannot be acknowledged, identified, or examined. They can, however, influence our moods and behaviors.

Now imagine another much smaller circle within the larger one. This circle contains the aspects of our inner world of which we are conscious. It represents the light of sweet awareness. As such, it presents the possibility for the constructive release of emotion and thoughtful examination of self, as well as an option for a conscious choice of behavior. Within this sphere we can note what is present and begin to willfully choose our behaviors rather than be ruled by the unconscious need for emotional discharge.

Next, imagine a little opening in that smaller circle that acts as a pathway from the unconscious self into the conscious self. This conduit is what eventually allows the unknown to become known. Unfortunately, if the pathway is very small (which it usually is), it is very difficult for the unconscious information to get through. Consequently, we need to stay focused on enlarging the pathway leading into the conscious self so our awareness of ourselves can expand. We do this by gently observing ourselves and having a willingness to welcome the information that comes forward.

Unfortunately, when unconscious information starts to come to light, we tend to become very anxious. This is because it can be primitive information that scares us and goes against how we like to see ourselves. We are not happy about seeing some of the aggressive, selfish, needy, or sexual parts of ourselves. In fact, we get so scared that we throw up a huge defense system in order to block out the material that is coming up. We deny and rationalize and withdraw from the new information, effectively blocking it from consciousness.

In our visualization we might envision this defense system as a wall or barrier standing firmly in front of the opening between the smaller circle and the larger one. This need not deter us, however. We can simply observe our movement to block incoming information, relax enough to let the new information come forward, and not judge it the second it comes up. We must stay centered long enough to take a look.

In this process we are not to favor our positive elements over our negative ones. Nor are we to favor our thoughts over our feelings or vice versa. We are to welcome them all, affording each inner element its rightful place in our consciousness. Our goal here is one of acceptance, one of integration, one of wholeness. As such, we are striving not only to become aware of each of our inner elements, but also meet them with open arms.

We must remember that our goal is not to be godly or perfect or pure. Our goal is to be whole. To achieve wholeness we must bring together all of our parts as one, embrace each one with benevolence, and move toward acceptance of ourselves as amazing human beings who carry within us every thought, feeling, and impulse that could ever exist.

This process requires us to develop an inner observer, which means that we must step back from our thoughts, feelings, impulses, and behaviors and study them in a detached manner. In our visualization, it could be seen as an all-knowing wise man or woman hovering above our two circles. Of course, this wise person is really an aspect of our self. He or she is nonjudgmental and is the part of us that solely watches what is going on. The wise person might sound like this: "Now I see myself pursuing this goal." "Now I see myself experiencing this feeling." "Now I see myself thinking this thought." "Now I see myself interpreting what just happened as meaning this." "Now I see myself engaging in self-attack." "Now I see myself behaving in this way." These observations help us to sort out the contents of our inner world by noting the specific elements of self and by positioning us above our daily drama rather than living within it.

A key element in coming to know ourselves is the ability to distinguish thoughts from feelings. Luckily, the inner observer is instrumental in helping us achieve this. It serves not only to differentiate between the two, but also allows us to work with them independently as each requires a different approach.

Here it can be helpful to imagine two columns. One is Column A, which is the feeling column, and the other is Column B, which is the thought/intellect column. The feeling column will contain a list of feelings that we are initially observing within ourselves as well as any deeper feelings that may underlie them. These feelings must be precisely named. We will not get anywhere by talking in generalities. For example, you should not simply say, "I feel bad." Exactly how do you feel bad? Do you feel betrayed, sad, angry, afraid, helpless, disappointed, unloved, lonely, abandoned, weak, disposable, unimportant, frustrated, rushed, misunderstood, and/ or embarrassed? The identification process must be very specific.

There should be absolutely no valuation or rational thought applied to the contents of this column. Its sole purpose is the identification of our feelings so that we can provide a good, understanding ear for whatever those feelings have to say.

Next, we must turn our attention to Column B (thought/ intellect), which allows us to start determining what we are doing to produce or maintain such feelings. Since our feelings have no ability to be rational at all, Column B is vital in bringing some cogent thoughts to the table. Here we want lots of valuation and rational thought — not harsh judgments, but an honest appraisal of how we are operating in ways that are not emotionally helpful to us. In Column B we are going to present ourselves with a list of things to reflect upon regarding the way we inwardly or outwardly function, knowing that upon changing these things, our feelings will most likely be very different. In Column B we may evaluate anything we want; however, there are several things that should be included. They are:

Transference/Old Memories
- What negative qualities and ways of being that were exhibited by significant people from our past are we transferring to innocent individuals in our current environment?
- Would it not be more helpful to attribute these elements to their original source and stop superimposing them on present-day individuals?

Perceptions/Interpretations
- What filters do we hold that alter incoming, present-day information?
- Are our perceptions distorted, limited, or selective?
- How does this create self-fulfilling prophesies for us?

Faulty Thoughts/Belief Systems
- Which of our thoughts/beliefs are incorrect?
- How are they incorrect?
- How are they affecting our emotional reactions to life events?

Expectations
- What are our expectations of certain people or events?
- Are our expectations too high, too low, or too immature?
- Are our expectations actually demands?
- How do others react to our expectations?

Current Behavior
- Is our behavior impulsive or thoughtful?
- Is our behavior too passive or too aggressive?
- Is our behavior constructive or destructive?
- Is our behavior in line with our goals?
- Does our behavior take both self and others into consideration?
- How do others react to our behavior?

Unresolved Inner Conflicts
- What unresolved inner conflicts do we have?
- Do we have a conflict regarding our worth, validity, or lovability?
- Do we have a conflict regarding assertion vs. passivity, success vs. failure, caring for ourselves vs. caring for others, love vs. hate, responsibility vs. irresponsibility, or dependence vs. independence?
- What events in life trigger our unresolved inner conflicts?
- How are our unresolved inner conflicts interfering with our happiness?

Deeply Embedded Character Traits/
Enduring Behavior Patterns

- What are our characteristic (and to some extent predictable) ways of behaving?
- Do we regularly engage in victim behaviors, self-sabotaging behaviors, aggressive behaviors, narcissistic behaviors, addictive behaviors, or irresponsible behaviors?
- Do we have an ongoing pattern of self-attack that leads to depression, shame, guilt, self-recrimination and self-loathing?
- How are these repetitive behaviors affecting our lives?
- Do they bring us consequences we would rather not face?

There will be some overlap in the above categories, which is just fine. For instance, transference is related to distorted perceptions. Distorted perceptions are related to faulty thoughts and belief systems. All three are related to expectations. In addition, unresolved inner conflicts are related to transference, perceptions, and behavior patterns. There is no need to worry about specificity here.

It is only when Column A and Column B are used together that can we successfully reach the goal of knowing ourselves. The two must be coupled, for neither is completely valid on its own. It is common in our culture for the feelings of Column A to be completely disregarded in favor of the rational thought of Column B. We need to avoid this mistake so that our efforts at emotional processing will not be sabotaged from the beginning. Nor in our great need to emote, create, and express should we be so critical of intellect that we do not use a most vital and spectacular tool.

To summarize our goals, they would look like this:

- Become more aware of self.
- Develop an inner observer.

- Learn to distinguish thought from feeling.
- Allow, acknowledge, and name feelings.
- Allow and acknowledge thoughts. Notice and correct any errors in thinking.
- Foster an attitude of wholeness, integration, and compassionate acceptance for all parts of self.
- Become familiar with current behaviors and enduring patterns that interfere with happiness.

Chapter 2

OBSERVE YOURSELF

In our quest for self-awareness and wholeness, observation of the self is essential. Observation of that which is going on within us is a hugely powerful tool in working through our emotions and in gaining control over our inner processes. The act of observation allows us to become aware of whatever we are thinking, feeling, or doing. It permits us to reflect on these things and then enables us to address whatever needs to be changed.

Observation gives us the opportunity to bring light to what was previously hidden in the darkness of our unconscious. It also gives us an opportunity to consciously choose how we will behave rather than behave reflexively as unwitting servants of own unacknowledged thoughts and feelings. It takes us away from blind, automatic functioning and moves us toward inner control and mastery of the self. Observation is extremely important in helping us achieve our goals.

To observe means to watch or to witness. In order to successfully watch, however, we have to stand separate from that which we are observing. We cannot stand right in the middle of the milieu, one with every thought, feeling, or desire. In order to correctly watch, there has to be distance between the observer and the observed. This distance allows for detachment. It allows us to have a respite from the rigors of constant thought, feeling, and desire. It allows us a modicum of peace.

So how do we do this? We can start by closing our eyes, breathing in a relaxed fashion, and taking note of the thoughts that go through our minds. As we watch, we need to make a point not to follow our train of thought. For instance, if there is the thought "I must remember to write my report," we can acknowledge the thought, but not keep ruminating about the report or about anything related to the report. What we are trying to do is to avoid engaging in linear thinking (logical thinking, building one thought upon another).

Linear thinking sounds like this: "I have to finish my report. I think I'll rewrite the introduction. It's too long. While I'm at it, I'd better check the whole thing for grammatical errors. It would probably look more professional if I had it bound. Yeah, that's what I'll do. I think I'll also have five copies of it made. I'll go to a print center tomorrow and get it copied and bound. I wonder what they charge for binding." Instead, we just need to watch the thought "I must remember to finish my report," allowing it to come and go. That is it; we must not go beyond that one thought. Then we need to sit quietly until the next thought comes up and do the same thing. Watch it come and go. This is the act of observing — noticing something, but not engaging in a string of thoughts about that something.

In our efforts to observe our thoughts rather than link one thought to another, we may even have an opportunity to observe ourselves trying not to think linearly, or we might detect a thought about how difficult this seems at first or about how we hope we are doing this correctly. None of what parades by is a problem as long as we do not turn our original thought into an ongoing stream of related thoughts. If we notice ourselves doing so, we need to gently return our attention to whatever we are observing.

The same sort of observational process can be done with our feelings. We can carefully acknowledge and welcome whatever feeling presents itself without getting carried away on a raging river of emotion. We can serenely pay attention to it with no emotional involvement and no thought as to what we are eventually to do with it. Right now we are just watching and being neutral.

We can do the same sort of observation of our physical bodies. We can either get a general sense of our bodies or we can put our attention on our individual body parts and quietly become aware of them. We can see how each part feels. We can note what is tense and what is not. We can even invite each part to relax. Of course, we need to refrain from getting off point with linear thinking about our body issues or health concerns and keep our attention focused on watching.

Observation of self is not limited to noting the contents of our inner world. We can also use our inner observer to view our behaviors in the outer world. We can take note of how we interact with others, the way we present ourselves, our ways of being, and the choices we make. Although we may eventually choose to alter our behaviors based on what we are seeing, we should avoid judging ourselves during the observational process.

Our inner observer is the most detached and most stable of all the elements of self that we have considered. It plays the role of the benevolent parent to an endless stream of disjointed, clamoring thoughts and feelings that run on and on unabated. It is the only constant in the bunch. As such, it is an extremely valuable part of ourselves, and we should strive to utilize this part of ourselves as much as possible.

Chapter 3

UNDERSTANDING CORRECT
SEQUENCING

The part of us that is centered on the experience of feeling is sometimes referred to as the emotional self, and the part of us that is centered on thinking is referred to as the rational self or cognitive self. Neither is superior to the other as they are both needed in order to reach our goal. However, if we want to successfully work through our emotional disturbances and achieve the kinds of behaviors that we want, the emotional self must be attended to first.

As mentioned earlier, there is a tendency to quickly skip over the emotional self and go directly to the rational self when attempting to work through an emotional difficulty. This is like trying to fix a broken arm by putting a cast on our leg. This is not to say that there are not tremendously helpful things that the rational self can provide, but it simply cannot come first in our efforts to get past a difficult feeling. Listening to feelings from the emotional self must always take precedence if we are to have success and achieve our goals of emotional release and behavioral control.

This is the case because the emotional self wants nothing to do with the rational self until the former is first heard and understood. It does not respond to lectures, evaluation, criticism, logical thought, impatience, facts, or advice from the rational self.

It only responds to heartfelt acknowledgment and understanding, i.e., good listening. When it gets the message from the rational self that it is being unreasonable, the emotional self feels rejected, abandoned, ashamed, unacceptable, despondent, angry, used, and conditionally loved. It then refuses to cooperate. This is because nothing rational can be heard when there is a heavy emotional charge in play, particularly when it is compounded by another's judgment. The head of steam must be discharged first; rationality can be accepted secondarily.

After the emotional self has been worked with, then it is on to the rational self. Here there is a gold mine of information for our use. The rational self will lay out all the facts, evaluate the situation, and come up with potential solutions. It will help us examine all the things about our inner and outer worlds that need examining. It will help us assess whether or not we are perceiving reality correctly. It will help us challenge our expectations. It will assist us in determining how our beliefs impede us. It will help us get responsible for our part in a given matter. It will differentiate what is good for us and what is not. It will evaluate and analyze just about everything.

Given the individual talents of these two aspects of our inner world, it is easy to see why one of our goals must be integration and wholeness. Without our rational self, the emotional self would run amok, and without the emotional self, the rational self would be barren. When the two are married, they make a great team.

To be absolutely clear, it needs to be understood that processing our emotions before consulting our thoughts is necessary, but not because the emotional self is nonsensical and must be humored along until the real thing arrives on the scene, i.e., the rational self. This is important to understand because many of us truly believe that rationality is king. However, this is not a helpful or accurate way to view things.

Deference to our thoughts is not our end game. While it is true that we must become aware of our thoughts and thought processes, we will find that upon examination, they are not always on point. They can be quite distorted at times.

We will also find that many times an idea (a thought) may sound good on paper, but when it comes to acting on it, it may not have validity if the emotional timing is not right. For instance, it may sound like a good idea to volunteer to help the needy; however, if we are emotionally drained and need to take care of ourselves for a while, it no longer qualifies as a good idea. It is the emotional self that carries the wisdom here. Or perhaps accounting sounds like a good idea for a major in college, but emotionally we are more suited to arts and sciences. Perhaps our emotional side knows we cannot sustain four or five years in a field we dislike. Here again, the emotional self weighs in with valid input.

So please do not misunderstand the need to process the emotional self first as an effort to shut up the emotional self in favor of a better part of us. The reality is that the rational self provides us with potentially good ideas and the emotional self lets us know whether or not we can emotionally sustain these good ideas. After consideration is given to both parts of self, a good decision can emerge.

Chapter 4

KNOW YOUR FEELINGS

In order to successfully process our emotions, we have to have a firm awareness and understanding of our feelings. We also have to be able to distinguish them from our thoughts. To this end we will take a look at the nature of feelings and how to distinguish them from thoughts.

The term *feeling* is derived from the verb *to feel*. In order to feel, we usually have to experience a physical sensation first. We either have to see, hear, touch, smell, or taste something in the external world or experience a biological sensation from within such as hunger, satiation, fatigue, or vitality. A biological sensation from within would also include feelings based on hormonal levels, organ dysfunction, disease, brain chemistry, or physically induced pain. Upon experiencing these external or internal stimulating events, we derive some sort of emotional response based on whether or not the stimulus was pleasant or unpleasant. These emotional responses are called feelings.

The need for direct physical sensation, however, is not always the case. Feelings can also be brought about by the workings of our mind. They can be created by our thoughts, beliefs, imaginings, expectations, perceptions, interpretations, and memories. When these mental processes are altered, our feelings tend to change in response. This affords us the possibility of achieving a modicum of control over our feelings rather than being hostages of our own machinations.

Whether our feelings are sensation based or the product of our mental processes, our feelings are linked to the arousal of the nervous system, are largely biochemical in nature, and are reactive rather than initiating. They are said to be reactive as they are tied to our sensory experiences, physical state, and the mental mechanisms which trigger them.

Because our feelings are reactions to random stimuli, they do not follow a line of rational thought. Instead, they are subjective, non-linear, and illogical. Consequently, feelings have gotten a bad reputation. They are often characterized as being mercurial, imprudent, unreliable, silly, and immature. They are also seen as having little value and should be eschewed in favor of logical, rational thought.

While our feelings are usually associated with the conscious perception of emotion, they can be present, yet remain within the realm of unconsciousness. For instance, we may feel very hurt about something, yet remain unaware of it while engaging in symbolic behaviors that belie its presence (irritable, punitive, or withdrawn behaviors). This lack of conscious awareness coupled with seemingly irrational behavior further contributes to the perception that feelings are unreliable and undesirable.

Yet our feelings are our heartfelt, honest response to life. They reside in the part of our brain that has no capability to do anything other than react. This part of the brain has the emotional maturity of a three-year-old and is totally dependent on the executive part of the brain (the part that deals with thinking and planning) to give it correct information, protect it, and guide it. Without the help of our executive center, our feelings have no way to be anything other than what they are.

Consequently, the emotional self must be viewed as a three-year-old child that we adore and dearly wish to protect. We must see the child as being young, impressionable, sensitive, expressive, spontaneous, and emotionally rich. We must see this young life as being dependent on us for limit setting, behavioral guidance, education, protection, validation, and kindness. We must also see this child as being dependent on us to feel wanted, special, accepted, and acceptable. But most of all we need to see the child as being dependent on us for empathic listening and compassionate responses.

There are several ways we can help ourselves where our feelings are concerned. The first thing we can do is to correctly identify or label them. We must give a name to whatever is present; for instance, we may be experiencing anger, hurt, disappointment, sadness, helplessness, fear, disgust, confusion, loneliness, or emptiness. This is not a thinking exercise, for we cannot identify a feeling with logic. It is a checking exercise. We need to turn our attention inward and check to see what we are experiencing. We are looking for a felt sense. That means we are trying to get a sense of what is emotionally going on. We are trying to detect something, to recognize it, to get the gist of it. We are looking for an emotional element of ourselves that we can describe. Under no circumstances are we to think when trying to identify a feeling.

The second thing we can do to help ourselves is to process our feelings correctly. Processing our feelings means working through them and handling them properly. In order to process them correctly, we have to listen to them without judgment or evaluation of any kind. More than that, we have to understand how our feelings came to be as they are. We have to acknowledge whatever it is that we have endured in life or struggled with that may have given rise to our current emotional state. We have to be willing to tenderly embrace the part of us that is in pain. We have to hear it and comfort it as though we would hear and comfort a child. Never must we evaluate, judge, or chastise ourselves for how we feel.

Once our feelings have been identified and given a compassionate hearing, they tend to quickly dissipate. They release not because we have done anything difficult or complex, but simply because we have granted them loving attention. Much of the time, this is all we need to do.

It is a bit counterintuitive to say that delving into something rather than turning away from it can bring relief, yet it is true. Working through our emotions is effective in that it allows for a release of inner tension similar to the feeling of relief we experience when someone has finally heard us and that what we have had to say has mattered. Attempting to circumvent our feelings, silence them, or ignore them is ineffective. We have to move through the darkness to get to the light.

There are times, however, when we have correctly identified and lovingly received a particular feeling and it does not release. Perhaps we feel anger that keeps churning. Or maybe we feel a sadness that feels too big to ever go away. This can be indicative of unidentified, secondary feelings.

What we need to know here is that there are oftentimes other feelings behind the ones that have first been identified. These secondary feelings also need to be identified. For example, if we are stuck on anger, there is a good chance that we are also feeling afraid, helpless, sad, hurt, disappointed, embarrassed, unwanted, or unloved, to name a few underlying feelings. If we are stuck feeling sad, there is a good chance that we are also feeling angry, afraid, alone, and helpless. If we are stuck feeling rejected, there is a good chance that underneath we are feeling angry, powerless, scared, misunderstood, and alone. We need to identify as many of these secondary feelings as possible. Then our primary feelings will usually release.

This need to attend to layers of existing emotion is not to imply that we have to wallow in our painful emotions, scare ourselves, and depress ourselves. It simply means that for a moment we must experience, acknowledge, and identify our feelings. It only takes a minute or two, and it can bring us great inner peace.

Naming our feelings is not only helpful in gaining a greater sense of inner peace through the release of inner tension, but it also allows greater behavioral control, which can bring positive experiences into our lives. Since our unacknowledged and unnamed feelings run our behavioral show, it is helpful to usher them into consciousness so we can start behaving appropriately. It has been said that what we can name we can tame, and this is so true.

A word of warning is due here. Oftentimes we think that we are having a feeling when actually we are having a thought. For instance, we might say "I feel that it's not right that the government is overreaching." This is a judgment, an evaluation, and/or an opinion. It is not a sensation you are experiencing that would qualify it as a feeling. Just because we use the phrase "I feel" in a sentence does not mean that a feeling is being expressed. In fact, any time we are attempting to express a feeling and the word *that* is in the same sentence, we are definitely not expressing a feeling; we are expressing a thought.

If we are expressing our actual feelings regarding governmental overreach, we might be saying "I feel frightened" or "I feel angry" or "I feel helpless." On the other side of the issue, we might be saying "I feel supportive," "I feel thrilled," or "I feel comfortable." Whatever it is that we feel, it must be stated in a one-two-three format: One, use the word *I*; two, say the word *feel*; three, insert a one-word expression of emotion.

It is also possible to circuitously express a feeling by saying "I feel like . . . and then insert a descriptive phrase. For example, we could say "I feel like I have a weight on my chest" to express feeling stifled, overwhelmed, or oppressed. Or we could say "I feel like I can't get out of this mess" to express feeling helpless, trapped, or restricted. We could also say "I feel like I did when I almost drowned" to express feeling terrorized, desperate, or hopeless." We could say "I feel used up" to express feeling exhausted, exploited, and/or resentful.

In all these examples we have started with a descriptive phrase and then factored it down to specific feeling words. This is an indirect route to identifying our feelings, but it can still be productive if we keep going until we end up with a word that best describes our emotional state. We must be sure, however, to move beyond our initial descriptive phrase in order to get the desired result.

If we have successfully done this and find that we still struggle with intractable feelings, we will have to commence working with our thoughts to see how they are informing our feelings. Our thoughts tend to have quite an impact on our impressionable emotional self and regularly upset the living daylights out of it. We might also take a look at some of our other mental processes (transferences, perceptions, beliefs, expectations) to see if they are generating distorted information that is upsetting to the emotional self.

At this point, we should be feeling much better, but if we are not, we would have to look further, not so much at individual feelings, but at our underlying character structure, our enduring patterns, and/or unresolved issues. For example, we would have to look at the possibility that we may be achieving secondary gains (payoffs) by holding on to certain feelings. Perhaps we are punishing others by continuing to hurt. Perhaps we are avoiding something. Perhaps we are struggling with guilt and feel like we need emotional punishment to balance the scale. We could also have attachment/dependency issues, masochistic tendencies, narcissistic leanings, unrealistic standards of perfection, self-esteem problems, victim consciousness, or fear of success. The list of possibilities is too long to address here, but we need to be aware of them in our quest for emotional balance.

There is a special breed of feelings that we have not discussed yet, and that is intuitive feelings or gut feelings. Intuitive feelings are feelings that provide information that we cannot recall having learned. When we have an intuitive feeling regarding a particular situation, we can understand that situation immediately without information derived from either conscious memory or conscious reasoning. This is because the memory that provides that information remains out of the range of our conscious awareness. However, it has been unconsciously processed and readied for retrieval in the form of a gut feeling. In such instances we are drawing our conclusions from the unconscious recognition of certain memories, meaning that our intuition is essentially information gained through our past learning experiences. These gut feelings bring a heightened state of awareness, are on target, and should be heeded, for we are inadvertently recognizing patterns and/or viewing the situation from a higher perspective rather than concentrating on the microcosm.

Some think that intuition is derived from our basic instincts. However, this is a bit different from the above explanation of intuition as a byproduct of learned behavior. Our instincts could be defined as an innate inclination to react in a stereotypical manner toward a particular set of stimuli (as opposed to learned behavior). They are usually primal survival instincts coming from our reptilian brain in connection with our right brain, and they are devoid of conscious reasoning. While it is best to examine our primal instincts so that we do not engage in destructive or inappropriate behaviors, at times our instincts can serve us well in matters of survival. Sometimes when there is an instinctual urge to watch out or to run, it is best to pay attention.

Intuitive feelings are experienced at a visceral level, which is why we call them gut feelings. Basically, our intuition acts as an information carrier that arouses emotion. It brings a heightened sense of awareness, provides a quick recognition of truth, and stimulates emotions that are appropriate to the situation. For example, if our intuition tells us that something is not quite right, feelings of dread, wariness, or fear will be brought forward. If our intuition tells us that all is well, feelings of comfort and safety will come forward.

The concept of gut feelings may seem confusing in that there may be no immediate thought or memory that explains their presence. However, when they happen, they present with certitude and are completely devoid of confusion. Their message is crystal clear. They speak of inevitability, of prescience, of knowing. The message they bring forward is correct and is not to be ignored.

Unfortunately, too often we ignore our gut feelings due to the fact that we start questioning them rather than accepting them as truth. While it is a good thing to examine our feelings rather than act on them impulsively, it is not a good thing to rationalize away our gut feelings. This is why it is so important to be able to distinguish between our sensation-based feelings, our thought-induced feelings, and our gut feelings.

Sensation-based feelings are experienced as moving, sentimental, lush, responsive, emotive, passionate, flowing, demonstrative, arousing, changeable, tumultuous, impulsive, and intense, but they do not carry a sense of certainty, of recognition, or of knowing. Thought-induced feelings are experienced similarly to sensation-based feelings but carry an element of variability as they change whenever we change our thoughts. Nor do they carry an element of recognition, knowing, or certainty. In fact, they can be very misaligned with reality. Intuition-based feelings (gut feelings) do not feel particularly sentimental, demonstrative, or passionate. Nor do they change. They are an accurate representation of reality. They can feel powerful, intense, and grounded, and they definitely bring a sense of certainty and recognition. A gut feeling is experienced as truth, as a clear message from within. It provides quick, perceptive comprehension of a given matter and will get this message across with an appropriate, related feeling.

When we are confused about whether we are having "regular" feelings (sensation-based or thought-based feelings) or intuitive feelings, it really comes down to what we do with our lack of clarity. If we are unclear about whether something is a gut feeling or "regular" feeling, it is better to err on the side of self-protection rather than spend inordinate amounts of time trying to figure things out. If something does not feel quite right, we cannot afford to take chances with our well-being, waiting around until we can identify what is amiss. If something nags us, we must protect ourselves first. We can figure things out later.

Whether sensation based, psychologically induced, or intuitively inspired, our feelings are helpful to us in so many ways. They temper the sterile quality of our thoughts. They open the heart. They are a tremendous source of energy when acknowledged and lovingly received. They warn us with their presence, tone, and intensity when we are getting off track. They provide emotional support for our goals. They guide us into areas of interest and success. They are effective in letting us know what we can and cannot sustain. They are the bedrock of our courage. They help us to turn aside abuse. They shake loose our defenses and let us know how we honestly feel about certain relationships or situations. They carry messages from our intuition, channeling intuitive knowing through gut feelings. They warn us of danger and of unhealthy situations. They help us denote the need for boundaries and assist us in instituting and maintaining them. Finally, they release us from self-recrimination by bringing us intuitive knowledge about why certain life events played out as they did. When attended to with care and consideration, the emotional self will do all this and more.

Chapter 5

DECODING THE
EMOTIONAL SELF

Sometimes it is difficult to determine what the emotional self is trying to convey because it tends to speak to us in code. One of the ways it does this is to use our physical bodies to get its message across. The most obvious of these tactics would be to cause physical pain such as headaches, stomachaches, neck pain, back pain, or heartburn. The emotional self can also cause us to have tics, spasms, or muscle twitching. It can even cause us to become accident prone, bringing us pain through injuries to our body. In a more subtle vein, it can show itself through our general physical health. For instance, we may be run down or subject to illness because we are not emotionally taking care of ourselves.

The emotional self can also be experienced through our heart rate, blood pressure, or heart rhythms. It can be experienced through intestinal distress, skin conditions, and hair loss. Additionally, it can manifest itself through our sleep patterns such as insomnia or hypersomnia.

The emotional self can also present physically by allowing our muscles to be relaxed or tense. A good test of our emotional state is to see if our bellies are soft or hard, meaning we can note whether or not we are tightly holding our stomachs in or letting them be slack. The first usually means negative feelings such as distrust, anger, fear, powerlessness, frustration, dissatisfaction, embarrassment, or vulnerability. The second usually means that we are comfortable, open-hearted, gentle, peaceful, and secure. Muscle tension in any part of the body indicates emotional distress. We can usually identify it by checking our bodies for areas of comfort or discomfort.

Along the same lines, we can check our adrenaline level to get an idea of what is going on with our feelings. If we are in a state of overstimulation as evidenced by nervousness, excitability, edginess, defensiveness, hypervigilance, hysteria, irritability, mania, or obsessiveness, this is a clear indicator of negative emotions. It can also signal anxiety or depressive states.

Another physical indicator of our feelings is our breath. We can observe our breathing and note its depth and speed. Is our breathing shallow, coming mostly from our upper lungs, or is it deeper, coming more from our diaphragms or our bellies? Is our breathing rapid or slow? Shallow, fast breathing indicates that we are in some sort of emotional distress (most likely fear or anger), while deep, slower breathing indicates a state of security and well-being.

In all these cases we can ask ourselves the following questions: "If this physical symptom had words, what would it be saying?" "What is my tic saying?" "What is my headache saying?" "What is my state of exhaustion saying?" "What is my breathing saying?" They are all trying to say something emotionally important if we would but hear it. While the specifics vary, much of the time they are trying to impart the message that either we are or are not happy with our current situation, choices, relationship, or life-path.

In addition to taking note of our physical state, we can also take note of our behaviors in order to determine what we are feeling. It can be particularly helpful to take a look at the nature or quality of our behaviors (negative or positive, aggressive or benign, self-defeating or self-caring, self-absorbed or selfless). Once we establish their quality, we can more easily determine what feelings they are reflecting. For example, behaviors that are self-destructive usually indicate feelings of rage, self-loathing, and powerlessness. Individuals engaging in defiant, oppositional behavior often feel angry, anxious, invisible, unheard, powerless, used, pressured, or burdened. Perfectionistic behavior can reveal feelings of fear, grief, powerlessness, and unworthiness. Even simple behaviors like a loss of temper, bouts of nastiness, a tendency to blame others, or a loss of patience are indicative of something that we are feeling.

Another way to gain awareness of our feelings is to become familiar with our motivations and intentions. If we can determine what they are, we are much closer to discovering our feelings. For instance, if we are motivated by power and our intention is to build an empire, we might be suffering from feelings of shame, worthlessness, weakness, or powerlessness. If we are motivated by the need for attachment and our intention is to find a relationship, we may be feeling needy, lonely, or afraid. If we are overly motivated by independence and our intention is to stand completely on our own, we may be holding feelings of fear, outrage, and frustration over having been controlled, used, or abused when in a previous state of dependency.

In determining your motivations and intentions, you might ask yourself, "What do I desire?" "What do I need?" "What would help me feel more comfortable or satisfied?" "How do I intend to supply myself with what I want and need?" "What sensation is propelling me toward my goal?" All of these questions can be helpful in revealing not only your motivations and intentions, but also the feelings that underlie them.

Yet another way that we can decode our emotional self is to observe and monitor our moods. We can take note of our current attitude, disposition, and outlook. Specifically, we can note the quality of our mood (pleasant or unpleasant, positive or negative, benevolent or malevolent), its intensity (strong or weak, resistant or yielding), and the direction it seems headed (ramping up for action or moving back to emotional equilibrium).

Our dreams can also be helpful in decoding the emotional self. While dream interpretation requires a bit of training, we can at least determine whether our dreams carry an overall feeling of anxiety, if they are sexual in nature, or if they are explosive and aggressive. We can also take note of what wishes we fulfill for ourselves in our dreams.

The emotional self can also be heard in the tenor of our communications with others. It is possible to realize how we are feeling simply by listening to the tone of our voice or the way we are speaking to people. Do we sound whiney or upset? Do we sound harsh or loving? Are we critical or demanding? Do our words show patience or impatience?

In a related vein, we can reveal our emotions by paying close attention to our self-talk. We can determine quite a bit in the feelings department if we just listen to what we are saying and how we sound when we talk to ourselves. If we find that we are speaking to our self in a kind and supportive manner, we are most likely imbued with positive, benign feelings. If we notice that we are saying hateful, judgmental, or denigrating things to ourselves, this is our cue that we are experiencing anger. We may think we are angry with our self, but in most cases we are angry with someone or something outside of our self and are now redirecting that anger inward instead. We need to acknowledge that anger as well as determine who or what originally triggered it. Then we can be appropriately angry with that person or situation instead of our self; we will notice an immediate improvement in the quality of our self-talk.

Once we have decoded our emotional self through any of the aforementioned methods, we will most likely have managed to come up with at least one initial feeling that we are experiencing. This is wonderful; however, we cannot stop there. We cannot stop because under our initial feeling there will be another feeling and then another and another. They will all be related even though they exist in separate layers (much like the layers of an onion). When attended to properly, each will release and move us closer to peace. In our quest to keep the decoding process going, let's take a look at some of the underlying feelings that usually reside beneath our initial feelings.

There are a variety of hidden feelings that can underlie an initial feeling; however, there are four main feelings that dominate. These are fear, sadness, helplessness, and anger. Much of the time they are present in combination. Let's take a look at each individually, starting with fear.

Fear is one of the most universal, commonly held feelings there is. It usually presents as a general feeling of dread or alarm, but in actuality can encompass a variety of individual concerns and trepidations. When addressed, individual fears are easier to identify and work through compared to addressing generalized fear. Consequently, in our efforts to discover our deeper feelings, it can be helpful to identify some of the specific things we fear.

One of the specific things we most fear is the fear of loss. In economic situations there can be the more obvious fears such as loss of money, power, status, security, options, respect, image, control, or comfort zone. In interpersonal relationships there is often a fear of loss of love and all that it entails such as feeling adrift, alone, lonely, needy, unsafe, unworthy, unlovable, disposable, and abandoned. In almost any arena, we may experience the fear of disapproval, which can leave us feeling irrelevant, inept, humiliated, discounted, punished, misunderstood, victimized, exposed, criticized, berated, vilified, or cast out.

Another kind of specific fear that we may experience is the fear of being consumed, taken over, or controlled by others in our environment. While this can occur simply because of another's incessant and/or unreasonable needs, expectations, and demands, most of the time it goes further than that. Usually our fear of being consumed is the result of an environment in which chaos, abuse, and pathology are present. This situation is extremely toxic for us, and we feel trapped within its grasp.

Examples of this type of environment might include living in close proximity to an active drug addict or alcoholic, a physical or emotional abuser, a "rageaholic," a mentally ill person, a law breaker, a control freak, or a narcissist. Within these situations we can develop a fear of exploitation, out-of-control people, upending chaos, imminent rage, and physical harm. We also fear falling apart, going crazy, crying incessantly, being trapped, having no choices, or certain death. We may also develop a fear of intimacy, an inability to trust, or a fear of commitment. The fear of being consumed all comes down to a fear of having to endure the unendurable and not knowing how to escape it or effectively deal with it.

Another explicit fear that we have is the fear of failing. When we fail, it becomes evident that we are imperfect and/or we do not have total dominion over the world. As ridiculous as the possibility for perfection or total control sounds, we still attempt to achieve it. When it becomes evident that we cannot achieve it, we end up feeling exposed as a fraud and then experience either a loss of self-esteem or the esteem of others. It goes without saying that accepting our human imperfections and limitations of power would be a much better route to take; it is both compassionate to the self and automatically eliminates a host of fears.

Yet another identifiable fear that we may have is the fear of our own rage and any impulsive actions we might take based on that rage. When we have been through a great deal of emotional trauma and are in a high state of internal rage, we can feel a bit murderous. This does not mean physical murderousness (although in extreme cases it could be), but having a feeling of wanting to wring someone's neck or shake some sense into them, beat the living daylights out of them, or leave them flat. We can also fear the fragmentation of self that can occur when our rage is out of control and we can no longer hold ourselves together. Here we no longer feel cohesive as a person; we feel like we are breaking apart.

Finally, when we find ourselves in a high state of rage and that state is unacceptable or abhorrent to us, we can also fear punishment from within ourselves. If we have not acknowledged and accepted our capacity for outrage, we may be subject to inner punishment from our conscience that will punish us with guilt, shame, self-recrimination, and anxiety.

The second major feeling that often underlies the first feeling we have identified is sadness. There are so many things over which we have grief. We are sad because of losses we have taken, over things we have never gotten around to doing, over things we wish we had done differently, over opportunities we have squandered, or opportunities that were not afforded us. We are sad that we did not stand up for ourselves sooner. We are sad that we did not treat people as we should have. We are sad over things that we have had no choice but to accept. We are sad over our loved ones' inability to see us, hear us, or understand us. We are sad that at times we have had so little physical or emotional support. We are sad that we have been injured so badly, that we have been gullible, or that our awareness has been so dismal at given points in time. We are sad that we are getting older, that our time on earth is limited, and that with aging, our opportunities are diminishing. We are sad that we have had times of self-absorption, of acted-out anger, of deep fatigue that robbed us of quality interactions with our loved ones. We are sad that we have to struggle, to work so hard, to always keep pedaling. We are sad over so very many things.

The third major feeling that often underlies our first identified feeling is helplessness. Helplessness is so difficult to feel because when it is in play, there is truly nothing we can do. Losses are about to be taken, and that is that. Even if we have all the intelligence, influence, and capability in the world, something is going to be lost or fail to go right.

Helplessness is related to the feeling of powerlessness. When powerlessness is in play, there may be something that can be done to improve the situation, but we do not have the power to make it happen. Perhaps we do not have the money to hire a better doctor or a competent attorney. Maybe the people involved cannot hear us or choose to discount us. Maybe we live or work with an oppressive person who restricts us from doing whatever we could have done.

One of the main things we are powerless to do is change others if they do not choose to change of their own accord. Unfortunately, we cannot help them "see the light" until they are ready to. Despite our excellent communication skills and heartfelt intentions, we cannot make others hear us or understand us if they have no ability or inclination to do so. Nor can we change others' perceptions of us if they do not wish to examine those perceptions. If we try to help them, they will most likely interpret our efforts as attempts to control them and will not alter this perception. Whether we are attempting to help others stand up to abuse, overcome an addiction, recognize a self-defeating pattern, or become more responsible for themselves, we are playing a losing game. We are powerless to walk their path; we can only watch.

On a grander scale we are helpless to stop change itself; we are unable to influence the universal cycles of life and death. These realities are difficult to face, but the sooner we can accept our own helplessness and/or powerlessness in certain areas, the better. Here, acceptance is crucial. It is also imperative that we develop a willingness to embrace the positive side of change. Change does not have to equate to catastrophe, particularly when we are attuned to our own strengths and capabilities.

It should be noted that both helplessness and powerlessness are tied to sadness because of the losses that surely will be taken. They are also tied to anger because we almost always have a layer of anger when losses present themselves.

The fourth major feeling that can underlie other identified feelings is anger, which can range from annoyance, frustration, and irritation on the low end of the scale all the way up to rage. Many feelings have anger in tandem. Some of the feelings that have an anger component are feelings of rejection, betrayal, hurt, abandonment, disappointment, sadness, frustration, and helplessness. Any time we feel controlled, exploited, victimized, abused, discounted, neglected, denied, or thwarted, there will be an anger component. When we feel misunderstood, unheard, unsupported, invisible, criticized, berated, or punished, there will be anger. When we feel scared or unsafe, we will also be angry. Feelings of resentment also hold anger. Whenever we fail after great effort, we can feel angry. When we find ourselves in a state of depression, we are definitely angry. When we feel anxious or panicky, we are oftentimes holding anger. When we feel stupid or unmasked in some way, we get angry. Likewise, we should expect anger when we feel guilt, shame, or humiliation. When we feel stifled, suffocated, or micromanaged, we feel angry. When we feel loathsome, worthless, or self-destructive, we are angry. When we feel overdone, long-suffering, or overly altruistic, we will feel anger (particularly if we feel taken for granted or unappreciated). When we have been untrue to ourselves, denied ourselves, or consistently put ourselves last, we will be angry. This is an incomplete list, but you get the idea.

Interestingly, anger is usually the first identifiable feeling to enter our awareness. Oftentimes we have no problem seeing it. In fact, it is common to get stuck on our anger, never getting to the layers beneath it. Unfortunately, this anger does not release if we fail to see what is beneath it. It just grinds away, we remain uncomfortably inflamed, and after a while the people around us get tired of our "anger junkie" routine.

Sometimes, however, when we really need to acknowledge our anger, we are blissfully unaware of it (particularly if we have already started acting on our anger). There are a few reasons for this. First, when we swing into action, we are generally not feeling anything. We are too busy acting. In fact, the more we act, the less we feel. We may be yelling and screaming or punching someone, yet fail to feel a lick of our own rage, sadism, disdain, or lack of concern for the person we are assaulting. If we did, we would probably stop. But we cannot because our state of action has blocked all emotion.

Secondly, if we are depressed, which is predicated on anger, our depression acts as a numbing agent (kind of like a shot of Novocaine™ to our brains). This numbness is pervasive and stops us from feeling much of anything except the excruciating pain of our depressive state. It anesthetizes all the feelings we need to work with in order to get rid of our depression and prevents healing through the correct channels of acknowledgment, identification, compassionate acceptance, and release. So not only do we have no idea that we are angry when we are depressed, but we are also clueless about the rest of our emotional entourage.

A third reason we sometimes have difficulty finding our anger is that, for many of us, it is considered a particularly bad feeling to have. Our parents, teachers, and religious groups urge us to be kind and loving. Anger is looked down upon. Consequently, we go out of our way to hide it from ourselves. We may go so far as to say that we are annoyed or irritated, but we hesitate to say that we are angry and almost never admit to being enraged.

A fourth reason we lose track of our anger is that, in our society, we take so many illegal psychotropic drugs that serve as anger suppressants or even go so far as to ruin our ability to feel good on our own. Those drugs hold feelings still instead of allowing them to vibrate, move, and release. Trying to get feelings to release in an active drug or alcohol user is like trying to fight city hall.

Fifth, our psychological issues can mask our underlying anger rather well. On the surface these issues do not seem related to anger at all. For example, who would think that panic attacks have anything to do with repressed anger or that we are stuck in the house with agoraphobia because of our anger? Or who would think that the doting, supermom is depressed because she is angry? Who would think that self-loathing or guilt is related to anger? Who would think to link anger and hyperactivity? Not too many. Our mental health issues need to be deconstructed so that we can find their emotional basis.

Sixth, sometimes when our anger is repressed, the rest of our feelings are repressed as well. Then we are in a fine mess. Even though anger is deemed a negative emotion, it is vital to our emotional health that we unearth it, entertain it, and honor it for a little while. We need to hear its message. While we do not want it hanging around forever, without it we can get stuck in a world of hurt.

Chapter 6

KNOW YOUR THOUGHTS AND THOUGHT PROCESSES

We will start this chapter with a few words on thoughts and then move on to an exploration of thought processes. Specifically, we will take a look at how our thoughts and thought processes can either help us gain mental clarity and emotional stability or interfere with correct thinking and inhibit emotional stability.[1]

When we speak of thought processes, we are referring to our mental or intellectual practices. These are also known as cognitive processes. Here we are looking not only at what we think, but also the way that we think, i.e., the way we arrive at our thoughts. Our thought processes are the inner mechanisms of our psyches that prepare us to assess and deal with reality. They can be on track or not, so it is imperative that we get to know them. We do not want to lapse into incorrect ways of thinking and make cognitive errors.

Thoughts

A thought is a consideration, reflection, or idea that is the product of mental activity. It is usually associated with intellect, reasoning, imagining, evaluation, judgment, opinion, memory, rationality, and objectivity. It is linear by nature in that one thought generally links to another and forms associations. It is the part of us that we use when making rational decisions.

Thought is very unlike emotion. It is not something that we experience so much as it is an activity that we do. As such, it is not reactive, but initiating. Thought is the part of us that feeds our emotional self the information upon which it reacts. This makes our thoughts very, very important. We are obligated to use them wisely.

When we consult our thoughts in order to temper the irrationality of our emotions, we are looking for a helping hand in the form of calm logic, solid facts, good ideas, new ways to view things, and judicious planning. We are also looking for a helpful evaluation of our behaviors, our perceptions, our beliefs, and our expectations. After our mental input, we can come away feeling more objective about the situation and far less emotive. Passion gives way to level-headedness.

Thought Processes

Sometimes after consulting our thoughts, we do not come away feeling better because our thought processes are not accurate or reliable. When this occurs we most likely are not interpreting our environment correctly. Old memories and/ or unresolved issues may be coloring our ability to see clearly. Moreover, our thoughts and beliefs may be too distorted or limited in scope to give us a reliable reading on reality. If this is the case, our judgments and evaluations will be incorrect and our expectations out of line. These difficulties with our thought processes can be brought to our attention and corrected. They will be discussed in detail below. The first mental process that we will explore is that of perception.

Perceptions

To perceive means to become aware of, to know, or to identify by means of the senses.[2] It involves recognition, discernment, interpretation, and understanding of the environment. Because perception is an individualized interpretation of incoming information, it is a highly subjective process. As a result, our perceptions can lead us to either a correct interpretation of the environment or to a distorted or incomplete understanding of the environment and then to faulty conclusions. These faulty conclusions have little to do with reality.

There are three main ways that we can misperceive incoming information. We can distort it, we can limit it, or we can selectively choose what information we want to see. All three of these possibilities are explained below.

Distorted Perceptions/Mental Filters

Distorted perception is all about altering incoming information into something other than what it originally was. One of the main reasons we sometimes end up with distorted perceptions is that perception is a mental process by which the nature of an object is recognized through the association of a memory.[3] This means that when we experience a new event in the present, old memories are triggered (because the new event seems similar to the ones in memory), and now the old memories tell us how to interpret the present situation.

In these situations our old memories act as filters that distort the new, incoming information. They promote the assumption that since something happened a certain way in the past, certainly it will happen that same way again. Here we are transferring data about yesteryear to a fresh, new moment, which may or may not have brought the same experience as that of days gone by.

This is similar to a beam of white light shining through a colored filter. As the beam of light approaches the filter, it is still white, but the minute it goes through the filter, it comes out another color on the other side. If the filter is blue, for example, we then give ourselves the information that the new event will yield blue. Then the emotions react accordingly. Unfortunately, the emotional self is reacting based on bad intelligence from a distorted perception.

This sort of thing is very self-destructive, not only keeping us from enjoying new experiences in the present moment, but also causing us to create self-fulfilling prophesies. If, for instance, someone does something nonthreatening in the present moment, but our memory-laden filters inform us that it is threatening, we might react to that situation poorly, perhaps even suspiciously or aggressively. We may engage in behaviors that are negative, blaming others or treating them as if they are going to judge us or hurt us. This will, in turn, bring us an unpleasant response from an innocent party who now feels misunderstood or maligned. We then feel justified in our original interpretation even though we have created that whole incident singlehandedly.

Distorted perception is particularly damaging in our relationships. We all carry forward memories of painful interactions with significant individuals from our adult or early years that we regularly and wrongly attribute to our present-day partners. This causes a world of hurt for our misunderstood, maligned partners who are sullied by our memories, convictions, and accusations. It also brings pain to us as we chafe under our convictions of wrongdoing and/or reap the angry, hurt reactions of our innocent partners.

When dealing with distorted perceptions/mental filters you need to ask yourself:

- Am I willing to acknowledge the fact that most of my stress comes not from my environment, but my interpretation of it?
- Am I willing, *to a reasonable extent*, to take responsibility for creating my own reality?
- How is the significant person in my present different from other significant individuals who hurt me in my past?
- How does it benefit me to keep turning my present moments into a rerun of my past?

Limited Perceptions

Distorted perceptions are but one way that we can misperceive our environment. Another way that we misperceive and thus misinterpret our environment is to engage in limited perception. This means that we take in partial information about a new situation and then interpret the present moment based only on that. This can happen when we are overly absorbed in our own wants, needs, anxiety, or depression, thereby effectively shutting out an awareness of what is going on with other people.

For example, we may interpret other people's fearful behavior as being aloof or standoffish, we may interpret their disappointment or sadness as being rude disinterest, or we may interpret their attempts at self-care as being selfish and rejecting. Obviously, we bring ourselves much pain with limited perception when a greater sphere of awareness could bring us peace of mind. We should always look deeper and have at the ready an array of possibilities for why something is or is not happening rather than seize the first, limited possibility.

Some questions you can ask yourself when dealing with limited perceptions are:

- Am I too focused on my own wants, needs, and moods to see clearly what is going on with others?
- Am I carrying anger that is blocking my ability to see other possibilities?
- Am I too attached to my suffering/victim status to see mitigating possibilities?
- Am I afraid to acknowledge a wider scope of incoming information because I might see something I do not want to see?
- How will it hurt/help me to widen my range of possibilities as to why others behave as they do?

Selective Perceptions

Another way that we misperceive our environment is through selective perception. This is based on justifying preexisting beliefs. When we engage in selective perception, we tend to select incoming information that supports what we already think and ignore or quickly forget possibilities that contradict our beliefs. Here we see things only within our frame of reference, our existing value system, and our existing belief structure. This maladaptive practice is a very restrictive and biased way to view the world.

Selective perception in not limited to our perceptions of others. It can also be applied to us. For instance, it can result in only selecting incoming information that supports a self-denigrating view of self no matter how many positives abound. Or it can result in only selecting information that validates us as righteous and blameless people.

Selective perception occurs quite a bit in the political arena where incoming information is selectively chosen to support preexisting beliefs. It is also in play each time we engage in sexist or racist interactions where incoming information is selected to support our preexisting ideas about how others will behave. *This does not apply to situations in which everything has been fairly considered and others are objectively exhibiting certain traits or behaviors.* Specifically, it is vital that we not get so caught up in trying to be open, inclusive, and cognizant of stereotyping that we miss what is actually happening.

Selective perception can also occur more benignly in situations where we are not attempting to justify our preexisting beliefs, but tend to see only the things we are currently thinking about, focusing on, or interested in. For example, it can occur when somebody buys a new car and now all he or she notices on the road is the same make and model as the newly purchased car. Or it can occur when a woman is pregnant and now all she sees are other pregnant women. It can occur when someone is focused on physical fitness and now tends to see physically fit people or perhaps people in need of physical fitness.

Here you could ask yourself:

- Is there more that I could be seeing and taking into consideration? What is the broader picture?
- Are my beliefs so rigid and dogmatic that I can no longer give consideration to incoming information?
- How is it helping me to assume that I am always right about my evaluation of others or of myself?
- Do I hang on to some beliefs because I am afraid of new possibilities?
- Do I have an egoistic need to be right?
- Is it possible that the beliefs I hold now may not apply to all situations for all time?
- What will I have to feel or address if I stop selecting incoming information that continually supports my own beliefs?

Beliefs

Another mental mechanism we employ is that of belief. A belief is an opinion or conviction based on an enduring thought that we embrace and deem to be true. It may be constructive or destructive, valid or invalid, but it is compelling by nature and powerfully affects our emotional state.

Our beliefs usually lead to an evaluation of that which is before us. Some result in a positive evaluation and others do not. When our beliefs are expansive, well informed, benevolent, and mature, our emotional reactions to our environment tend to be benign. When our beliefs are rigid, narrow, malevolent, or immature, they can result in particularly harsh or judgmental evaluations of self and others, which inform our feelings and thereby cause negative emotional reactions to our environment.

We might think of the impact of a belief as a simple A, B, C formula. A is the stimulus/incoming information, B is our belief along with the mental assessment it generates, and C is our emotional and behavioral reaction to that belief and associated mental appraisal. B resides between A and C, exerting influence. Within this context, belief (B) is the strongest power player for it is not so much the stimulus/incoming information (A) that dictates our emotional and behavioral responses (C) so much as it is our intervening beliefs (B). When B changes, C changes.

Consider this example: If a two-year-old child spills a glass of milk (A) and his or her parent holds the belief (B) that two-year-olds are coordinated enough and attentive enough to consistently hold on to a glass of milk, that parent will most likely be upset, critical, and angry (C). If that parent holds the belief that two-year-olds are developmentally uncoordinated and inattentive, that parent will have a more understanding, compassionate reaction. Here the key to emotional balance is in realizing what belief is in play and what valuations ensue. Fortunately, we can become aware of our beliefs, question them, and provide ourselves a better alternative.

The questions you might ask yourself regarding beliefs are similar to those listed under selective perception. However, since here you are not necessarily trying to defend your beliefs, you might expand the questioning to include:

- Is it okay for me to not know everything?
- Am I willing to educate myself on certain matters?
- Do I even know what my beliefs are or am I on automatic pilot?
- Am I afraid that if I have to reconsider some of my beliefs, I will have to relinquish some that I think are valid? Who says I will have to relinquish those that I think are valid?
- Am I afraid that if I reconsider my beliefs, I will lose control of a particular situation?
- Do I feel better or worse when considering a new belief?
- If I let go of a particular belief, can I stand my feelings if something emotionally uncomfortable presents itself?

If not, what would make me think I cannot tolerate an uncomfortable feeling for a little while?

There are a few widely held beliefs in particular that are both erroneous and misleading. These are based on myth or misconception, and if adhered to, can result in tremendous emotional upheaval. Four of these fallacious beliefs are listed below.

Heaven's Reward Fallacy

In this mode of maladaptive thinking/believing, we expect our self-sacrifice and self-denial to pay off in the end. Then we feel upset, victimized, and bitter when it does not happen. These negative feelings are a direct result of not living in the present, of not including ourselves in life's equation, and of not staying attuned to ourselves.

Certainly there will be times when self-sacrifice is needed, such as when attending to very young children, assisting with an infirm family member, getting through tough financial times, completing our education, or starting a new business. Yet even in these times of necessity, it is best to keep a close eye on our own physical and emotional state rather than wait for heaven's reward.

While our sacrifices and ability to delay our gratification will hopefully pay off (and they sometimes do), we should not entertain the assumption that it is okay to sacrifice endlessly. The ability to delay gratification is a good thing, but masochism is not. We cannot barter with the universe, trading self-sacrifice for future rewards, or we may end up with precious little left of ourselves.

Here you can ask yourself:

- What feelings am I ignoring each time I make a sacrifice for another? Why am I ignoring these feelings?
- What might happen if I go ahead and make choices for my own welfare?

- Would it be impossible to tolerate another's reaction if I did choose for myself?
- Can I live without another's approval or understanding? If not, why not?
- Have I imperceptibly graduated from normal giving to overgiving?
- If I stop overgiving, will something in my life spin out of control? If so, might it be better to deal with this reality directly rather than through continued overgiving?
- If my situation is legitimately dire and requires my continued service to others, can I give to myself in small but meaningful ways and/or devise a plan to consistently move my own interests forward?

The Fallacy of Change

The fallacy of change leads us to believe that we can get others to change if we just love, serve, lecture, suggest, explain, cajole, or pressure them enough. Here we do not respect the sovereignty of others. Our happiness is dependent on whether or not others will modify themselves.

This need for change we are talking about is far beyond healthy communication between individuals who are attempting to work and live together harmoniously by discussing things that get in the way. These kinds of discussions are necessary. They help us get along. They are not based on our worth or lack of it. It is our attempt to change others so that we can feel worthwhile that is the problem.

It is particularly enticing to try to get someone to change where others have already tried and failed. We mistakenly think that if this person will change for us, we must be special. We also unconsciously believe that if they change, we will feel vindicated, heard, understood, chosen, worthwhile, valuable, and validated. The problem is that others do not change unless they want to. However, we refuse to believe this, opting to pursue the fallacy of change.

Attempting to change others is a particularly destructive pursuit because we feel so much worse about ourselves when they do not change for us. Moreover, we waste so much of our lives trying to effect change where change is highly improbable or downright impossible.

Here we need to take our focus off changing others and replace it with a focus on making our own choices and establishing our own boundaries. Additionally, we need to ask ourselves what responsibility to ourselves we are avoiding by constantly paying attention to other people's business. You could ask "What truths do I not want to face about my current situation?" "What truths do I not want to face about myself?"

The Fallacy of Control

When entertaining the fallacy of control, we either believe incorrectly that we are victims who are externally controlled or that we are hugely powerful in our ability to control things. Neither is correct.

In the first scenario we feel constantly victimized as we focus on others doing things to us, when, in fact, there are decisions that we could be making to influence the situation. Here you need to ask yourself:

- What fears or convictions do I hold that keep me in a passive position?
- What would happen if I confronted my fears and made a life-altering choice?
- What might happen if I am more assertive in communicating my likes and dislikes to others?
- Am I getting a payoff through remaining a helpless, hapless victim?
- What is this helping me avoid?

In the second scenario we assume responsibility for everyone and everything as though we actually control the thoughts, feelings, and behaviors of others. This can be a carryover from our earliest days when we felt merged with our mothers and felt a powerful sense of omnipotent control.

Here you can ask yourself:

- What anxieties would I have to face if I let myself know the truth about not being able to control others?
- Do I really believe I am so powerful that I can control every event in the universe?
- Can I tolerate feeling somewhat separate from others as the reality sinks in that we are not one?
- Will feeling separate from others kill me?
- Is there an advantage in not being tied so closely to others?
- Might it be healing to accept the fact that everyone has limitations?

The Fallacy of Fairness

The fallacy of fairness occurs when we believe that life is fair. Sometimes it is tied to the heaven's reward fallacy in that we do what we consider to be the right thing thinking that we will eventually be rewarded for our good behavior. Thus, life will have been fair.

The fallacy of fairness is a tricky one. This is the case because whether or not a belief in fairness is considered a fallacy rests on one's viewpoint. Perhaps the most accurate assessment of the situation might be that life is unfair as viewed from the lower levels and fair as viewed from the upper levels.

If viewed from a cosmic level that takes all actions into account throughout the eons, there may actually be an overall fairness to life. According to this belief system, when times are tough and life seems unfair, we may be working off our karmic debt or helping others balance theirs. Or perhaps if viewed from the perspective of life's difficulties being opportunities for growth and development, life may be seen as fair. It may even be considered fair if assessed from the perspective that we are creators who do not have a full awareness of our own creative abilities and thus regularly generate negative, "unfair" situations for ourselves without realizing our own part in the matter. Likewise, life may be fair if it is true, as some believe, that we choose our own parents, siblings, significant others, obstacles, life path, and growth opportunities before we incarnate on this planet and are just living out what we have set up for ourselves.

Such an expansive belief system can be very helpful at times, particularly if it used as an adjunct to our real feelings rather than as a form of denial. However, despite the possibility of an overarching, cosmic fairness, we do live on the lower realms, and that reality must be faced. We must acknowledge and accept the fact that on the lower levels, fairness is oftentimes not discernable. Nor does it directly and clearly follow positive action. Rather, it is unpredictable, failing to follow our earthly timetable. It may not exist at all.

If we view our lives from a very limited perspective, as most of us do, we cannot possibly believe that life is fair. Life on this planet is a free-will zone. We can create anything we want. Many times we get caught in the crossfire. People do not even know that they are creators who are creating one thing or another every minute of their lives. On top of that, we are subject to certain laws on this planet that restrict our power. We can only do so much. Some have said in jest that this planet is the reform school of the universe. Sometimes it looks like that. Narcissism is rampant. Awareness is dismal. Everything is a struggle. Stress weighs us down, clouds our vision, robs our energy, and toys with our emotions. The list could go on. So yes, life here is a mess, and if viewed from a myopic perspective, it is definitely unfair. In fact, it is unfairness on steroids.

If we deny this reality and insist on seeing life on planet earth as potentially fair, we are going to be in for some pretty uncomfortable emotions. Trying hard over and over yet failing to receive fair treatment is anger producing. It can leave us feeling consciously or unconsciously resentful, bitter, or enraged. Sometimes it leaves us feeling forsaken and bereft. At the very least it can leave us with a sense of betrayal or hollow disillusionment when unfairness continues to dominate the scene and our reward does not emerge as expected. It is much better to embrace reality and good naturedly adjust our expectations.

As always, the best thing to do under these circumstances is to stop focusing on what we think *should be*, and focus on what *is*. Then we must ask ourselves, "What do people with this reality do?" Generally speaking, what *is* on this planet is that things are slow going, difficult, and unfair. What do people with this reality do? They do the best they can, they try to view things more expansively, they tap into their reservoir of spiritual and creative power, they accept what they cannot control, they create responsibly, they live by their own principles, they are inner directed, they refrain from comparing themselves to others, and they certainly do not lie to themselves about a fairness motif on this particular, dense planet.

Whatever the case, you must ask yourself:

- What, if anything, am I doing in exchange for reciprocal fairness that I would not ordinarily be doing?
- Would I be doing anything different if I knew there was not any fairness, or am I doing what I do simply because I choose to do it?
- If I am doing what I choose to do without thought of reward, is it okay to forget about what others do or do not receive for their efforts and live my own life?
- Is my outrage over unfairness stemming from too much focus on others and what they have or have not given me for my efforts?
- Am I giving to get?
- How do others feel about being pressured to give back?
- Could I change my locus of control to more of an internal one rather than an external one?

- Is it enough to live my life by my own internal standards even if fairness does not ensue?
- What fears must I face if I am to acknowledge the reality that I do not control the universe with my goodness?
- When unfairness presents itself, can I refrain from taking things personally?
- Is it possible for me to see reality as my friend, rather than be blindsided by lies I have told myself about reality on this planet?

Judgments

As we have seen from the above discussion on beliefs, our beliefs and the evaluations that accompany them often lead to judgments about what someone should be doing, thinking, or feeling. These assessments are sometimes called *shoulds* ("You should do this. You should not do that"). *Shoulds* can apply either to others or to oneself. They are important enough to warrant a section of their own.

Shoulding that is applied to others typically involves a focus on something we think they ought to be doing, saying, thinking, or feeling. Here it is all about changing others. As such, it is a focus on something that we cannot control and needs to be replaced with acceptance, the relinquishment of a focus on others, and boundary setting for ourselves instead. We need to concentrate on our own goals, our own choices, and our own actions. Essentially, we need to mind our own business.

Shoulding that is applied to oneself usually involves a focus on something that we think we ought to be changing and/or improving about ourselves. This can be a positive thing to a certain extent, particularly if we have been inner focused, thoughtful, and compassionate with ourselves. It can be particularly helpful when we work to improve ourselves without the pressure of an overly critical inner observer or an excessively strict set of demands and expectations. Conversely, it is not helpful when we harshly evaluate ourselves, attack ourselves, or pressure ourselves.

Unfortunately, *shoulding*, as applied to oneself, may not reflect thoughtfulness, an inner focus, or a feeling of compassion for self. Instead it is about complying with something other individuals think we ought to be doing, saying, thinking, or feeling. While this can be helpful within the context of a friend, mentor, or loved one who is trying to give us constructive advice or feedback, it is mostly a negative thing. It is negative because no one ultimately knows what is best for us but we ourselves. It is also negative because it tends to be lacking in truth to self and is usually fear based.

Shoulding as applied to oneself can also have to do with internal or external pressure to become more aligned with generalized standards of conduct as set forth by religious, societal, political, or cultural doctrine. Again, barring sage advice or helpful feedback, only we know what is best for us.

Be aware that one's developmental stage is a factor here. A certainty that one always knows what is best for self does not always apply to the very young, particularly teenagers. Neither does it apply to those with oppositional or defiant patterns of behavior who are attempting to simply oppose authority. It also does not apply to vulnerable individuals caught up and swept away by certain ideologies. Nor does it apply to those who suffer from certain mental disorders or cognitive impairment. There are more exclusions, but these are the most obvious ones.

When it comes to *shoulding* as applied to oneself, the focus needs to be on self-reflection and self-assessment to determine if something would or would not be a positive thing for us to do. We must always strive toward an internal locus of control rather than an external one if we are to live in peace. This means that we need to focus on our own wants, needs, goals, and decisions rather than getting our direction and approval from external sources. More often than not, any losses that we take in refraining from following the crowd will be restored to us many times over.

In situations that involve *shoulds* for others, you might ask:

- How do I end up feeling when I try to change ot
  and they won't cooperate?
- What am I feeling that is making me want to change/
  control another's behavior?
- What is stopping me from setting healthy boundaries/
  limits for myself instead of trying to change others?
- Are my efforts to change/control others improving or
  harming my relationships?
- Have I respectfully communicated my wants and needs
  before communicating in the form of *shoulds*?
- Can I start moving to a position of dealing with what *is*
  rather than what I think *should have been*?
- Am I willing to ask myself what people with this
  particular reality do, and then do it?

In situations that involve a focus on ourselves, you could ask:

- What would it feel like or look like if I didn't abide by
  the *should*?
- What would it feel like or look like if I did abide by the
  should?
- What stands in the way of my abiding by the *should*?
- What law says I have to comply? Why should I comply?
  Do I want to comply?
- Can I prefer that something be a certain way rather than
  elevate it to a *should*?
- Whose voice is telling me what I should or should not
  think, feel, or do? Is it mine or someone else's?

Unrealistic Expectations

Unrealistic expectations are aspirations that have a low
probability of being fulfilled. They are related to *shoulds*, but can
spring from a variety of sources. We may have them because of
what we have had modeled for us. We may have them due to
low self-esteem or an overinflated sense of self-importance. We

1e to a lack of awareness or a lack of established
een self and others. We may have them because
nentally immature and/or naïve. We may have
re are narcissistic and self-absorbed. We may have
them... we have been overindulged. We may have them
because we cannot yet stand on our own. We may also have them
because we have some sort of mental illness that impedes our
ability to test reality and make sound judgments.

Expectations can be unrealistic in that they are either too
high or too low. We can ask too much of this world or too little.
Most of us associate unrealistic expectations with aspirations that
are too high, but it is just as unrealistic to expect that others will
respect us if we allow them to walk all over us. For example, it is
unrealistic to presume that if we selflessly serve others, they will
know what we want and need for ourselves. They will not. It is
also unrealistic to think that our abiding love will change others,
particularly without their intention to work on themselves. This
will only result in our getting used up.

There is a particular kind of unrealistic expectation,
however, that tends to consistently be too high and deserves
special attention. These are infantile expectations. They deserve
special attention because we all have them and we are usually
quite unaware of their presence. They are beautifully outlined in
Necessary Losses by Judith Voirst. [4]

Infantile expectations are unrealistic, self-absorbed
expectations that may have been perfectly appropriate when we
were infants, but no longer hold validity in the adult world. They
do not necessarily come from a place of willful self-centeredness
so much as from a lack of maturation. As such, they are benign
in origin, but can get in our way emotionally and behaviorally
nonetheless.

Some of these infantile expectations are "I have an expectation
that the world owes me a living," or "I expect to be perfectly heard
and understood," or "I expect to always be the center of attention."

Others are "I expect everybody else to consistently attend to me," and "I expect them to enjoy attending to me."

A common infantile expectation is that of unlimited power and control as opposed to the reality that we have limited power and control on this planet. Like our erroneous beliefs regarding omnipotent control, this expectation is tied to our experience in the womb where we had a supreme sense of authority that led us to feel very powerful in our ability to achieve need fulfillment. A related infantile expectation is that there will be a place of perfect comfort and safety in this world despite the fact that this ended with our emergence from the womb (our last bastion of perfect safety and comfort).

Another infantile expectation is that we must achieve grandiose standards of beauty and perfection rather than make do with a human-proportioned self. One more is the expectation that it is possible to achieve perfect communication when certainly it is not. Yet another is that it is not only possible but necessary to always garner approval. Lastly, we expect that it is both possible and acceptable to be exempt from recognizing and abiding by others' boundaries; we simply do not do well with the word *no*. This is usually related to the deluded idea that we are so amazingly special. All of these expectations turn into demands and evoke distressed emotional responses and behaviors from us when they are not met.

As with beliefs, we can note and alter our infantile expectations. Here are a few of the things we can do besides hanging on to our infantile expectations and then getting upset when others do not honor them:

- We can learn to accept what *is* rather than lament what *should have been.*
- We can ask ourselves what people with our particular reality do instead of continuing to demand what we cannot have.

- We can learn not to put our efforts into trying to change others.
- We can learn to focus on our own choices.
- We can learn to stay in the present rather than stay rooted in the past or obsess about the future.
- We can learn to flow with the universe, i.e., we can agree to accept change.
- We can come to understand the limitations on our power, i.e., we can learn to determine what we control and what we do not.
- We can learn to hear the word *no* without interpreting this to mean that we are unloved or that we have been diminished.
- We can learn to respect others' boundaries.
- We can give up the idea of perfection.
- We can understand that we will not always receive the response we want or the approval we want.
- We can understand that there is no such thing as perfect communication.
- We can accept the fact that we will not always be perfectly heard and understood.
- We can register the fact that there is no place of perfect comfort or safety.
- We can learn that it is okay to have a human-proportioned self rather than a bigger-than-life self.
- We can cultivate a sense of ordinariness in that we are all part of humanity and share in its joys and struggles.

When we notice that we are engaged in unrealistic expectations, we might ask ourselves:

- How is it helpful to supply my emotional self with the wrong information?
- How is it helpful to pressure myself with impossible expectations?

- Is it kind, thoughtful, or ethical to pressure others with my impossible expectations?
- Am I getting the results I want from imposing my expectations on others?
- Would others love me more or less if I lowered my unrealistic expectations of them?
- Do realistic expectations frighten me?
- Can I be content with just being ordinary once in a while?
- Can I survive without every single one of my needs being met?
- Can I fulfill some of my own needs?
- Can I possibly change my demands and expectations to preferences?

Memory

Another of our mental processes is memory. Memory is the ability, process, or act of remembering or recalling that which has been learned or experienced. The information or events that we remember are called memories. Memory is a multifaceted mental function that involves awareness, recognition, understanding, retention, retrieval (bringing stored material into consciousness), and interpretation or readout (subjectively decoding retrieved material). It is usually broken down into categories of immediate, recent, and remote memory.[5]

Our memories can be affected by many things such as previously learned responses, mental set (readiness to respond selectively to certain stimuli), fatigue, amnesia, organic lesions, physical trauma (concussion), drug use, aging, and psychological disorders such as depression, anxiety, dementia, and psychosis. They are prone to secondary elaboration by our other memories, needs, and wishes. Some memories may be partially or entirely blocked while others can be successfully retrieved. There are memories based on emotions experienced rather than on language, as in young babies. There are screen memories that act as barriers against other associated memories considered taboo. There are biological memories, which are inherited memories of how to react to certain stimuli. These memories lead us to follow certain lines of development. All in all, memory is a rather complex matter.

The thing for us to keep in mind is that our memories are influenced by many factors. As mentioned above, they are prone to secondary elaboration, and so can be amplified or embellished, understated, or simplified. There is probably no way to know how accurate a memory really is, so the best we can do is observe our memories, realize that there may be more to them than meets the eye, and note the impact they are having on our lives. We can also process our memories by allowing them to come forward and respectfully acknowledge the emotion that is attached. This will decrease the emotional intensity of the memory.

Our interpretation of current reality is affected by our stored memories and the emotional charge that they carry. Even if it is years removed from a precipitating event, the feelings tied to a particular memory can remain very much alive. New experiences can trigger these old memories and emotions, and they can come rushing to the fore, causing us to associate them with our present-day experience. This is tremendously unfair to people in our current environment. In fact, our memories can color reality to such an extent that a rational evaluation of our situation can become very difficult.

However, once the memory has been observed from a detached viewpoint, the emotional charge has been given an opportunity for constructive release, and we determine how it is coloring our present moment, it becomes just another element of self to be worked with and understood.

For better or worse, memories are a powerful, influencing factor in the way we perceive our world. They are important in our evaluation of the self and they need to be worked with in a constructive manner.

When working with memories, we might ask ourselves:

- Is it possible to observe my memories without attaching to them?
- Can I allow my painful memories without acting upon them?
- Can I bring compassion to my painful memories?
- Is it possible to acknowledge certain memories without bringing judgment and recrimination upon myself or others?
- Can I allow my positive memories to heal me?

Transference

Transference is the term given when we attribute the qualities or characteristics of a significant person from our past to a person in our present. Then we react to the new person as though he or she is that someone from our past. It is directly related to memories which distort our perceptions. For example, if someone in our past was controlling, we would have a tendency to see a new person in our life as being controlling whether that person was or was not. Unobserved, this can be poisonous to our relationships. Who wants to be misperceived and mislabeled when that is not who he or she is at all? Nobody.

It is best to familiarize ourselves with the top two or three issues that were a problem for us with significant people in our past. Perhaps they were problems with control, neglect, emotional unavailability, paranoia, blame, lack of support, self-absorption, abusiveness, disrespect, disengagement, abandonment, untruthfulness, defensiveness, yelling, intimidation, invasiveness, narcissistic usage, passivity, smothering, disempowerment, rejection, etc. Whatever they were, we must get to know them as soon as possible and cease unconsciously attributing them to the wrong people. Once we have familiarized ourselves with these trigger points, there is much less chance that we could blindly attribute these characteristics to innocent people in our present day. There is also a greatly reduced chance of our reacting inappropriately.

Transference does not only happen when we transfer our thoughts and feelings onto persons in our present, but it also happens when we redirect our wishes onto them. This means that not only are we failing to see them for who they are, but we are now expecting them to fulfill our unmet needs and wishes as well. We expect them to do what the persons from our past did not do because, in our minds, the new persons represent the old ones.

Of course, this puts a lot of strain on any relationship, for new persons cannot and should not be responsible for filling all of our unmet needs. They are not wish-fulfillment machines. They are people in their own right with their own unfulfilled wishes, needs, and dreams. They are not here to be improved versions of our mothers, fathers, brothers, or sisters. Nor are they here to compensate for deficient relationships from our past.

There are probably people in our lives who love us, are familiar with our past, and do not mind going the extra mile to give us what we need, but we should view them as exceptionally compassionate, loving individuals who go out of their way to respond to us correctly. We should see them as blessings and not take advantage of their loving hearts. Never should we fault them for what they do not do, because what they have already given was a gift, not our just due.

Fortunately, transference is not always a negative occurrence. There can be positive transferences as well in which we attribute the positive qualities of people from our past to individuals in our present. This redirection of our positive thoughts and feelings can be nice for the recipients, but it does put a bit of undue pressure on them to live up to our expectations. It is always better to allow others to just be who they are, which gives them leeway to occasionally not be all peaches and cream.

Having a positive transference to someone can set us up for disillusionment when it becomes apparent who he or she actually is. This can be an unhappy circumstance for both parties as we may need to view the other person in an idealized manner and the other person may need to be loved for who he or she is.

After we have transferred certain positive qualities from persons in our past to persons in our present, we sometimes identify with them. We want to be like those persons and try our best to do so. This is fine as long as the persons we are identifying with are truly good role models and as long as we do not overdo it. However, it is not okay if they are persons other than who we think they are.

Regrettably, there are situations in which the persons we are identifying with do not actually have such positive qualities. We just think they do. Perhaps they are too aggressive, too self-sacrificial, too self-absorbed, too competitive, or too driven. They just look good to us because transference has been in play and, therefore, we are seeing them as we think they are rather than as who they really are. Here we need to look out and pay attention to reality. We can develop better qualities in ourselves without identifying with dubious people from our past or present.

There is also a form of projection that mimics positive transference in which we attribute our own positive qualities to others. Here we assign all kinds of virtues to individuals who do not necessarily possess such qualities. We are merely seeing ourselves in them. While this does not involve reassigning a quality from someone in our past to someone in our present, it is being included here because it transfers a specific quality from one individual to another. It also involves the possibility of viewing him or her in an idealized, unrealistic manner.

The questions we might ask ourselves about transference are:

- Do my feelings about a present-day person or situation belong to another day and time?
- Who or what do my feelings actually belong to?
- Is it fair to attribute my feelings to a person in my present?

- Can I acknowledge that when I react with emotional intensity to something or someone that this may be an indicator of transference?

When it comes to transferring our wishes onto others, we can ask:

- Do I want to remain a slave to my past, infringing on other people to fill my needs?
- Is it fair to use up others in my quest for need fulfillment?
- Do I want to miss the opportunity to know and love people in my present for who they really are?
- Do I want to remain a needy, self-absorbed child forever or do I wish to bring responsible, adult functioning to my present-day relationships?

Regarding identification as an extension of transference, we can ask:

- Who exactly am I identifying with?
- Why am I identifying with this person?
- Is this person worthy of my admiration?
- Can I cultivate some of this person's qualities without losing myself?
- Can I still love someone from my past, but know that I should not identify with some of his or her qualities and characteristics?

Black-and-White Thinking / All-or-Nothing Thinking

Black-and-white thinking occurs when we think in absolute terms such as *always, every, ever,* or *never.* In reality, very few events in human experience are absolute. When we find ourselves speaking in absolute terms, it is helpful to ask ourselves if there was ever a time when this was not the case. We might ask "Does this really *always* happen?" or "Does this really *never* happen?"

Black-and-white thinking is a bit infantile in nature, harkening back to our earliest days when we had no capacity to see both the good and bad in people or situations. Instead we split them up into all good or all bad. Normal human beings have both good and bad traits; they are not all black or all white. Life situations may sometimes be all bad or all good, but most of the time this is not the case.

Overgeneralization

Overgeneralization is related to black-and-white thinking and occurs when we apply sweeping generalizations to specific, individualized cases. Here again, we must ask ourselves if there was ever a time or a situation when it was not the way we are saying it will surely be. We can remind ourselves that just because a certain event occurred, this does not mean that X, Y, or Z will necessarily happen.

Disqualifying the Positive

Disqualifying the positive occurs when we continually refuse to acknowledge anything good. We insist on entertaining and cherishing negative thoughts and expectations regardless of more positive life experiences. Disqualifying the positive is sometimes done to guard ourselves from increased levels of anxiety and depression if we should take a chance on happiness and then things do not work out. It is a ploy to stay safely depressed at a manageable level rather than suffer a new disappointment and have to feel more pain.

Here we must ask ourselves:

- If nothing good counts, what, then, does count? In what way does it count?

- What is worse, the permanent pain of staying safely depressed or the temporary pain of a new disappointment?
- Is there a chance that I might not end up disappointed and could achieve a good result instead?
- Which way of functioning gives me a chance at happiness?

We could also make lists of personal accomplishments.

Jumping to Conclusions

Jumping to conclusions happens when we quickly decide that something has occurred or will occur even if there is no evidence to support this assumption. We make up our minds without checking anything out. We attempt to read minds and tell fortunes. Most of the time we jump to the conclusion that whatever we believe has occurred or will occur will surely be negative.

Here we need to ask ourselves:

- How do I know that?
- How do I know things will turn out that way?
- What evidence do I have to support A, B, or C?
- Am I willing to check out the facts?
- What other conclusions might I arrive at given the facts that I know?
- How does a hasty conclusion help me?
- Is a hasty conclusion helping me to keep negative opinions of myself alive and to solidify a self-denigrating and self-attacking position?

If we persist in jumping to conclusions, we need to ask ourselves what other issues may be in play.

Personalization

Personalization comes into play when we behave as though we have omnipotent control, assuming personal responsibility for things that are fully or partially out of our realm of control. It is based on a cognitive error, for certainly all events in life do not lead back to us.

Personalization is common in those of us who are overly enmeshed with others and therefore are not yet fully defined as separate individuals. This lack of self-knowledge and self-definition can result in boundary confusion, which means that we do not know where our boundaries end and where someone else's start. Another way to say this is that we are confused about whose likes, dislikes, desires, feelings, thoughts, moods, character flaws, goals, motivations, limits, perceptions, perversions, beliefs, and values are our own versus some else's.

Due to this boundary confusion, we are unsure what originates from within us and what originates from within others. We are unclear about whose fault things are. Given this boundary confusion, we personalize and end up taking responsibility for things that never originated from within us to begin with. It can be helpful to get very clear on who we are as individuals versus who someone else is. This clarity can be particularly effective in dispelling the guilt or sense of culpability that we experience when someone treats us poorly, does us damage, or invades our boundaries. Barring masochistic tendencies, rarely does the wish to be treated poorly or invaded or damaged originate from within us.

Sometimes we personalize to protect significant others because we rely on them. This is more likely to happen when we are young, underdeveloped, needy, dependent, and/or generally unable to take care of ourselves. Here our very existence depends on convincing ourselves that our caretakers are reliable, kind, capable, sober, and sane. If not, we tell ourselves that their behaviors surely must be our fault. In cases where our caretakers do not display these qualities, we may personalize to avoid acknowledging exactly what others in our environment are capable of being or doing. Sometimes we personalize in the hope that if we take others' responsibility for them, they will not harm us more than they already have. In such cases we must work to strengthen ourselves and our ability to thrive on our own so we no longer have to take on another's responsibility in order to survive.

When personalization is occurring, we must ask ourselves:

- How do I know that I am the one to blame?
- Who says I am the one to blame?
- Who or what else is involved in this situation?
- What unresolved issue, emotional vulnerability, misperception, anxiety state, depressive state, aggressive state, impinging belief system, active addiction, or mental disorder may be in play within the other person?

When dealing with personalization, we need to inquire of ourselves realistically how much of the responsibility for the problem is ours. We need to admit to ourselves that we do not have omnipotent power but instead face the fear, sadness, anger, and helplessness that come with that realization. We also need to get busy developing our own self so that reliance on toxic others is no longer a necessity. Also, we can enjoy the relief that comes with that.

Blame

Blame is pretty much the opposite of personalization. Whereas with personalization we take on all the responsibility ourselves, with blame we take none of it. Instead we assign all responsibility to someone else.

Impugning others in the form of blame is a way of shifting focus away from oneself. It is being listed as an error in thinking as it can result in an evaluation of the wrong person. Here we blame others rather than acknowledge that we may have played a part in a given matter. Or we blame them in order to find relief from our own painful feelings of fear, anger, sadness, and helplessness. This is very different from objectively assessing a situation, determining where something went wrong, and deciding how to remedy it or not let it happen again. Blame is different from honest assessment because it involves avoiding an unbiased appraisal of a situation rather than impartially looking at it. It also involves judgment and excoriation rather than compassionate acceptance of one's foibles.

Instead of blaming, we could look at our own behaviors as possible contributing factors. We could also be honest about what feelings we are trying to escape by changing the focus to another person through blame. The big question with blame is "What would I have to face within myself if my focus were on myself rather than diverted to another person?" This is not to suggest that we should always take responsibility for what goes on in our environment, but we do need to take an honest look at our possible contribution to a given situation, and certainly we must be responsible for facing and working through our own feelings.

Oftentimes our responsibility in a particular matter is somewhat ambiguous, passive, and/or inadvertent. This can be harder to own up to than a more obvious transgression. For example, we may have trusted where we should not have allowed another to take advantage of us. We may have given too much, stayed too long, focused too much on changing uncooperative persons or made bad choices out of loneliness, neediness, or depression. Perhaps we have continually chosen the wrong kind of partner, gone to a well that has been consistently dry, failed to truly see and understand someone, or have simply given up too soon. None of these are sadistic, unconscionable, or unforgiveable errors, yet we do have to take responsibility for them.

This is easier to do when we understand that taking responsibility for oneself and taking blame are not the same thing. We can be responsible for our own feelings about a given matter and have had absolutely no responsibility whatsoever for its occurrence (e.g., child abuse, a crazy boss, a sociopathic relative). Or, as mentioned above, we may have had a part in the matter but our part may have arisen from lack of awareness, passivity, weakness, or fear. Even if we do objectively think that we may have had a substantial hand in whatever happened, taking responsibility can be done with calm acknowledgment of the facts rather than by punishing, berating, and castigating ourselves. Taking on responsibility should not be synonymous with taking on guilt.

Sometimes we cannot take responsibility for our part in a given matter because others involved seem to have so much unacknowledged culpability for the situation. They have contributed mightily to our pain, and we believe our feelings about their part in the matter to be valid. We want these culpable persons to take responsibility for their part in the matter, but usually they will not. This makes it all the more difficult to look at ourselves because our hurt and outrage impede introspection. Instead, we may deny the offending parties satisfaction by refusing to assume a lick of responsibility.

Yet even with the knowledge that others have had a big hand in the situation, we still have to get ourselves a plan. We still have to get back up, figure out a viable pathway, and get going. This is taking responsibility in the sense that we are assuming responsibility for the trajectory of our own lives.

It can also be helpful to understand that the word *responsibility* means "ability to respond." We cannot respond to a situation if we have assigned responsibility for it to someone else. We think that once we have offloaded it to someone else, we are free to move on as though nothing ever needed to be examined or changed. But in reality our problem still remains. We still do not have a plan for change. This is because we are not able to respond if we have not first assumed responsibility for our problem.

When dealing with others who are clearly at fault in a given situation, we might ask ourselves, "Can I acknowledge the faults and limitations in others without being sadistic, cruel, critical, and insensitive?" Most people already feel bad about mistakes they have made. However, if a person is truly a threat to self, others, or society at large, then we should not worry about his or her feelings and take the necessary action to secure our safety and well-being. There are times when things need to be called out for what they are, and in these instances placing responsibility squarely on the shoulders of the perpetrator is indicated; there need not be concern for whether or not we are blaming.

Labeling or Mislabeling

Labeling or mislabeling occurs when we explain a situation by categorizing it rather than by describing the events of the situation. We label either ourselves or others in a negative, permanent way, and in doing so we change a behavior to an identity.

Here we should refrain from immediately branding someone as a jerk or an ass, and look at the possibility that there is something more to his or her behavior than meets the eye. We can ask ourselves if there could be a more positive or understandable meaning for what just happened. Or we could ask ourselves, "Is there another way of looking at this that could empower me or empower the other person?"

If we are the one being labeled, we could ask ourselves how exactly we are jerks, asses, etc. This way we can take things back to a focus on behavior and not on a global assessment of our self-worth. Even if we did engage in a negative behavior, we should remind ourselves that no one is perfect and that this is not an indictment of our overall personal worth. We all fail to succeed from time to time.

Magnification and Minimization

When engaging in magnification and minimization, we magnify the negative and minimize the positive. Instead, we might ask ourselves exactly how the situation is so bad or specifically how it is not good enough. If we are speaking of a person, we could ask ourselves how this person is not good enough, or how he/she is too much. Then we need to ask ourselves the question "Compared to whom or compared to what?" We could also ask ourselves the question "Is it all right for a person or situation to have good and bad elements?" "Does a negative quality have to destroy all other good ones?"

Catastrophizing

Catastrophizing is related to magnification and occurs when we focus on the worst possible outcome that will most likely be horrendous, intolerable, and/or insurmountable. We tell ourselves that it could well result in injury, death, financial ruin, or personal defeat. We believe that, at the very least, it would entail tremendous emotional suffering.

Realistically, in many of these cases discomfort may be involved, but certainly not catastrophic losses. Even if catastrophic losses were involved, this way of thinking keeps us from acknowledging our ability to effectively deal with and recover from loss.

Here we might ask ourselves what it is that could happen if we did have to tolerate a catastrophic situation. As with magnification/minimization, we could ask:

- What specifically makes this situation so bad? Compared to whom or compared to what?
- Would it be possible to accept a bad situation rather than fight against it?
- Might acceptance of a worst-case scenario free me to start focusing on problem solving for the situation and making constructive choices, given my new reality?
- Who exactly says that this particular situation would be intolerable or insurmountable?
- Do I want to take somebody else's word for it or do I want to create my own reality?

- Have others survived similar situations? How did they do it?
- Is starting over always bad?

Emotional Reasoning

Sometimes we confuse mental reasoning with emotional reasoning. In this process we incorrectly conclude that if something feels right, it must equate to a correct, logical assessment of the situation. For instance, we may think that if we feel unloved, we actually are unloved.

When engaging in emotional reasoning, we rely on our unexamined feelings to arrive at our assessments and/or decisions rather than on objective reality. While our feelings are important to consider in our assessments and decisions, by themselves they often do not have anything to do with objective reality. It is important to realize that just because something feels true does not necessarily mean that it is true.

Here we might consider interrupting our emotional pattern by asking ourselves:

- How can I believe that?
- What is in it for me to continue believing that what I am feeling is the truth?
- Am I sticking to my feelings because I am enjoying punishing someone?
- Am I enjoying punishing myself?
- What can happen if I continue to insist that my feelings are gospel? Do I want that?
- How will this help me meet my goals in this situation or with this person?

We must remind ourselves that it is okay to feel as we do; it is just not okay to ignore other aspects of reality. We must also remind ourselves that if we still feel this way when we have had time to think things through, we do not have to do anything we do not want to do.

At this point in our discussion of emotional reasoning, it is important to add a caveat. It is in regard to intuitive/gut feelings that can masquerade as emotional reasoning, but certainly are not.

Sometimes we have a gut feeling or intuition regarding a particular situation in which we can understand it immediately on an emotional level without the need for conscious reasoning. In such instances if our intuitive impression of the matter feels true, it probably is true. Here we are most likely drawing our conclusions from unconscious information stored in our memory banks or receiving helpful instinctual nudges from the reptilian part of our brains. No matter what their origin, our gut feelings are usually correct and should be heeded because we are probably recognizing valuable learned patterns or responding to our primal survival system.

It is vital that we learn how to distinguish between intuitive knowing and emotional reasoning as one is on target and the other potentially off-base. The ability to correctly rely on our gut feeling is quite different from being overtaken by an intense emotional state which we unquestioningly believe conveys the truth. The first feels more like a crystal-clear certainty, a knowing, an *Aha!* (whether about something good or something bad), which we realize without thought or excessive emotional agitation. This intuitive feeling can be very strong and definitive and can present as an emotional jolt once the truth of a matter is revealed. This may be a jolt of fear, disappointment, or horror on the negative end of the spectrum or joy, calmness, or relief on the positive end, but it carries certainty and does not produce the same feeling as a shaky conclusion arising from an agitated morass of unexamined feeling.

An intuitive feeling is an emotionally conveyed recognition of truth. It does not originate in our emotions. The emotion involved is simply a carrier of the intuitive information, with the intuitive feeling not carrying an element of judgment or self-recrimination. It simply brings straightforward information.

Emotional reasoning feels more like a conclusion born of emotional churning. It often has an element of blaming others or blaming self. With emotional reasoning the emotion produces a conclusion rather than acting as a carrier of information that has originated elsewhere. The uncertain phrase that usually accompanies emotional reasoning is "Well, it *feels* like the truth." This is infinitely different from the definitive statement "I know this is true." Here absolute clarity is one's indicator of truth.

Always Being Right

When attempting to always be right, we believe that no matter what, we must prove that our thoughts, feelings, and actions are correct. Being wrong is not an option, and we will argue interminably in order to demonstrate our rightness. The thoughts and feelings of those around us are ignored.

This may be related to our self-esteem, to our fears of powerlessness, to trepidation over being hurt, to a dread of belittlement, shame, or punishment, or to a conviction that the one who is right is the one who gets to live. The list could go on, but suffice it to say that there are many understandable reasons that we feel the need to fight in order to always be right.

Here we must ask the questions:

- Would I rather be right or happy?
- How is this stance affecting others?
- Will this stance help me get what I want?
- What will happen if I am not pronounced right by others?
- What will happen if I keep justifying myself until others finally, wearily give in?

Chapter 7

POSITIVE THINKING

Positive thinking is usually regarded as a good thing, but in reality it can be either a good or a bad thing. It is a good thing when it is accompanied by a truthful assessment of how we really feel and then used to introduce new, more hopeful possibilities. It is a bad thing when used to override or deny our true feelings. One approach uses positive thinking as a tool to uplift you after reality has been faced and the other uses it as a tool to contradict reality.

The manner in which we use positive thinking depends on how aware we are and how courageous we are in our ability to face uncomfortable or painful feelings. It takes great strength to let ourselves know what is present emotionally, and it is tempting to whitewash this reality with positive thinking. However, if we take the easy way out, eventually these whitewashed feelings will make themselves known through physical, emotional, or behavioral problems. If we can sustain it, it is better to take the courageous route and use positive thinking as a helpful, secondary tool rather than as our only tool.

When we choose to use positive thinking to override our true feelings, the emotional self feels as though we are trying to disregard it or that we are telling it lies. When upset, it usually cannot get behind too much positivity because it simply does not believe these things to be true. To the unacknowledged emotional self, positive thoughts are dissonant and misaligned with whatever it is experiencing. In fact, it perceives this action to be a blatant lack of attunement and a failure to listen. Unacknowledged emotion rarely responds to intellect, even if it is positive intellect. This is why it is better to acknowledge our emotional dynamics first and then introduce positive thoughts as an honest attempt to move our feelings to a better place.

As long as they are not used as an exclusive coping mechanism, positive thoughts can be very powerful in that they help us to shift our mental focus. They may be spiritual or philosophical thoughts that enlighten and uplift. They may be down-to-earth thoughts that introduce a practical new pathway. They may be reinforcing thoughts that remind us of our strengths. All of these positive thoughts can serve as affirmations and tend to be deeply sustaining. A particularly helpful positive thought is that there was never a winter that was not followed by a spring. Things will eventually get better simply by virtue of the movement of life's cycles. Also, holding the positive thought that we are safe and secure can be very beneficial. Another way to introduce positive thought is to count our blessings rather than our troubles. It helps to refocus us when we have lapsed into victim consciousness.

Positive thinking is somewhat related to correcting errors in our thought processes. This is because the process of identifying and correcting those errors is a mental pursuit that introduces a better way of thinking about things, but it is only tangentially related to feelings. Correcting errors in our thought processes can alter our feelings, but it does not directly attend to them. Consequently, we have to be careful how we use positive thinking. If implemented correctly, being on the lookout for inaccuracies in the way we think does not have to constitute blind positive thinking. When we use positive thinking as a secondary tool, it can allow us to observe our feelings, view them with compassion, assess the thoughts that underlie them, and then introduce a more realistic way of viewing a situation. In contrast, positive thinking used as our only coping mechanism does not involve observation, emotional attunement, or assessment, and solely attempts to shift the focus by introducing a new storyline.

Now let's shift gears and take a look at the role of positive thinking in creating our life circumstances. Whereas positive thinking is not always helpful as an exclusive method of dealing with uncomfortable feeling states, it can be consistently helpful in creating a better life for us. This is the case because thought is the cornerstone of creation, i.e., it initiates the creative process, and positive thoughts tend to result in positive creations. Of course, these positive thoughts need to be backed by our emotional support, the presence of clear intention, and then action in the physical world, but they provide the initiating principle that establishes the creative direction in which we are going.

When we think an initiating thought over and over, it takes root, it flourishes, it deepens, and it becomes hardy. This is much like a scratch on a wall that when scraped repeatedly with an object, creates a groove in that wall. Over time and with repetition, a single scratch turns into a created channel. Sustained thoughts are like this created channel. The more we think a thought over and over, the more we bring it forward into creation.

Since sustained thoughts lead to creative channels, it is important that we consciously choose our initiating thoughts. We have to be proactive with this, for it is definitely something we cannot leave to chance. Unfortunately, we have many repetitive, unconscious thoughts running through our minds that can also take creative form or, at the very least, create a negative focus for our lives. This is unfortunate and supports the idea that conscious awareness is necessary in order to create positive pathways in our lives.

It has been said repeatedly by those in the metaphysical world that thoughts are things, that they are the basis of creation, and that due to this, they should be carefully monitored. This is certainly true, and if we do not monitor them, we may end up creating things for ourselves that we do not want. It has also been said that the universe takes note of what we are interested in.[1] This means that if we are obsessed with thoughts of doubt, fear, lack, failure, and helplessness, we are eventually going to manifest these things in the physical world as a self-fulfilling prophecy. Fortunately or unfortunately, our sustained thoughts act as prayers that are answered.

Do we have to be afraid of every little thought that goes by in terms of its creative ability? No, because it takes a lot of concentrated, repeated thought to turn a scratch into a channel; otherwise we would all be genie's who could simply make a wish that would immediately come true. We would all have our heart's desire all of the time. So no, let's not be frightened of our thoughts or get obsessed with never uttering one negative thing. That gets old, not to mention that it makes us look ridiculously superstitious.

Besides, there is something called magical thinking that we all engaged in as children and certainly do not want to revisit now. This is the childish idea that if we think something, it will magically come true. If we are mad at mommy and wish she were dead, we believe that she will certainly die. We can store up a lot of guilt that way all because of an immature belief that was never true to begin with. Magical thinking has no relationship to the focused, creative process that we are discussing here.

Once the creative process has been initiated, it requires teamwork to push it through into manifestation. First is our initiating thought; we have to be able to conceive of something before we can start to create it. Then we have to have the intention to follow through on this thought. This means that we have to have a sense of purpose to reach our objective. This needs to be supported by our emotions so that we have the energy and desire to follow through; otherwise we will end up with conflicting intentions and our original creative thought will not get pushed through into the physical world. Finally, we have to do the work in the physical world to make our thought a reality. We have to put in effort. Nothing is going to happen otherwise, no matter how much or how positively we think about things.

The element of emotional support for our initiating thoughts is of particular importance in the creative process. Our ideas and our feelings need to be in agreement. If not, it will be difficult to keep the creative process going. The emotional self can be either an amazing support in the creative process or a terrible hindrance if it is not on board. This is why it is important not to go forward solely based on our positive thoughts, but on our positive feelings as well.

To this end, we have to consult ourselves quite honestly and see if we actually feel like doing this or that. If we do not feel at peace with it or if there is any sort of a drag on it, there is most likely a better path. We can always find a new, positive thought to create around, one that we can get behind, support, and sustain. Alternatively, we can modify or fine-tune our original thought or hold off on it for a while until the timing seems better or our circumstances have changed. Anything is better than trying to force ourselves to do something that we do not feel good about. As the old saying goes, "You can't fool Mother Nature." [2]

Finally, a last word about the feelings that accompany an initiating thought is in order. When we want to move toward a goal, it is very effective to allow ourselves the actual feeling of what it would be like to reach that goal. We need to feel the gloriousness, feel the relief, feel the power, feel the capability. That way thought and feeling can work in tandem toward manifestation. This is more than simply having emotional support for our goals. It is an active use of emotion that makes our goals more tangible and helps us bring them to fruition. We should not just think where we want to be. We must feel it as well.

Actively using our emotions to manifest our goals is somewhat related to being appreciative. If we are trying to create more of the things we want, we need to hold a feeling of gratitude and appreciation for all that we have. This is true even if, as yet, we have too little of what we want. We need to be grateful for our health, food, shelter, family, and friends. We need to be grateful for our job, our means of transportation, our freedom, our mobility, our senses, our talents, and the very air we breathe. The more that we feel appreciative, the more we will draw our intended goals to us. If we want the good life, we should consider keeping a gratitude list going at all times.

Chapter 8

KNOW YOUR DEFENSE SYSTEM

A defense is a mental mechanism that serves to protect us against an awareness of our own thoughts, feelings, and impulses. It acts as an inner barrier that shuts out personal information we do not wish to acknowledge. A defense system is simply the group of defenses that we use most often to keep ourselves in the dark.

Everyone has a defense system that impedes threatening elements of our inner world from reaching consciousness. Defenses vary from person to person, but they all serve the common purpose of protecting us from knowing things about ourselves that may cause us anxiety. These defenses are sometimes referred to as coping styles. While they may help us temporarily manage our anxiety about reality, they do not actually help us cope with it in the sense that we are dealing with it; rather they help us avoid dealing with it. So the term *coping* is a bit misleading.

The defense system has a formidable job. This is because the contents of our unconscious will not be denied. Its inhabitants demand satiation. They insist on a hearing and they force us to face reality. Consequently, they exert tremendous pressure on our defense system and continually push against its trying to break through.

When the contents of our unconscious cannot successfully emerge into our field of conscious awareness, we are left with a conflict that begins to cause us problems.

- It can make us physically or mentally ill.
- It can cause us to engage in behaviors we do not want to engage in (e.g., acting out).
- It robs us of our inner truth.
- It keeps us in unhealthy or damaging situations.
- It keeps us from our true purpose in life.
- It drains our energy.
- It delays our maturation and sometimes arrests our development.
- It deprives us of volition and control.
- It reveals us to be childish and immature as we live our lives acting stupidly, provocatively, nastily, narcissistically, etc.
- It gets stronger the longer we refuse to deal with what is.

None of this has to come to pass. The pressure from our defenses countering the pressure from our highly charged unconscious material presents an unnecessary conflict—one that would not have to be there if we would simply consent to welcome the unconscious material coming forward. Certainly we do not have to maintain such a stringent objection to experiencing reality, nor do we have to resist knowing our truth.

Many of us erroneously believe that it is our unacknowledged thoughts, feelings, and impulses themselves that are the cause of our difficulties. They scare us with their intensity and primitive content (aggressive, sexual, or infantile). We also believe that allowing them into consciousness is synonymous with acting upon them, which is not the case. These beliefs give us reason to keep stuffing the contents of our unconscious back down into the darkness. It gives us reason to disown ourselves, to judge ourselves, and to truncate ourselves.

The truth is, however, that the contents of our inner world are not the real cause of our difficulties. The real problem is our failure to allow that content entry into consciousness. The real problem is our objection to experiencing reality. The real problem is the judgmental, hateful reception we give our unconscious material when it does finally make itself known.

It can be quite freeing to know that our thoughts, feelings, and impulses are innocent. They are certainly not our enemies. It is also helpful to know that once allowed into our conscious awareness and appropriately observed, embraced, and understood, they become our allies. When such a welcoming reception occurs and an alliance is formed, the pressure behind our inner elements abates. Within our loving embrace, our thoughts, feelings, and impulses experience the comfort of acceptance and then are willing to accept the limits we must put on their expression in the outer world.

Given all this, we need to familiarize ourselves with our defense system so that we can recognize it and gently dismantle it when it starts to block information attempting to enter our field of awareness. With a little practice this is doable. There is certainly no need to bow to the demands of our defense system.

Defenses are roughly divided into two categories. They are primary (primitive) defensive processes and secondary (higher-order) defensive processes. Primary defenses act in a comprehensive, undifferentiated way, affecting our thoughts, feelings, and behaviors as a package. Secondary defenses tend to affect specific areas of thought, feeling, and behavior or some combination of the three. Primary defenses are carryovers from our younger years, specifically the preverbal years.

The following discussion of defense mechanisms reflects my own thought processes along with those of Nancy McWilliams as set forth in her book, *Psychoanalytic Diagnosis: Understanding Personality Structure in the Clinical Process.*[1] The primary defenses are listed below.

Primitive Withdrawal

Primitive withdrawal is the removal of oneself from a situation; it is a retreat, a departure, a checking out. This is seen in infants who, when overstimulated or upset, simply fall asleep.

The adult version of this is individuals who retreat from stressful social or interpersonal situations, eschew interpersonal contact, and avoid interpersonal problem solving. They tend to replace interpersonal relating with enjoyment derived from their own interests or fantasies. It has been said that these individuals like the space in between people more than they like people. As such, they may be more interested in philosophy, science, music, or spiritual pursuits. This defense is seen in people who experience their environment to be extremely difficult or emotionally unfulfilling. The upside of this defense is that, whereas it provides an escape from reality, it does not usually distort it. However, drug use to alter consciousness and avoid dealing with reality does fall in this category and can distort reality.

Denial

Denial is a refusal to acknowledge reality. This defense is also related to infantile functioning in that when something objectionable is happening, the infant simply refuses to accept that it is in fact occurring. The adult version is similar. Adults simply rewrite reality in their heads convincing themselves that if they do not acknowledge reality, it is not happening. Overly positive people, people who refuse to mourn, people who engage in magical thinking ("If I don't go to the doctor, nothing will be wrong with me."), people who refuse to acknowledge addiction or abuse, people who refuse to acknowledge their physical limitations, and people who will not be honest about their relationships all qualify as deniers.

Omnipotent Control

Omnipotent control refers to the belief that we have totalitarian power and control, which gives us dominion over all things. Like primitive withdrawal and denial, it is related to infantile functioning. Infants feel merged with their environment for a while. They have an unbounded sense of power and control and think that all things that happen occur because they made it happen. The adult version of this defense is "If you set your mind to it, you can do anything." With all due respect to the power of thought, this idea is bereft of all practicality and reasonableness. This defense counters feelings of helplessness and vulnerability. It is the stuff that empire building is made of. The thought that we can simply assert our will and control our environment is an intoxicating one, but not a realistic one.

Primitive Idealization (and Devaluation)

After infants outgrow their omnipotent control phase, they enter a phase of idealization in which their caregivers are imbued with omnipotence. They desperately need to believe that someone is invincible, benevolent, all-knowing, and in charge. This belief in a strong, protective caregiver keeps their anxiety at bay. The adult version of this is idealizing our partners, doctors, bosses, politicians, spiritual leaders/gurus, social group, and celebrities. We even idealize our own personal views and tastes. We think that in order to be safe we must attach to idealized people or ways of being rather than face our fears and develop our own strengths.

When it becomes apparent that our idealized others or ways of being are not perfect and cannot always keep us from harm, we soundly devalue them and run to the next idealized person or way of being. We refuse to entertain the reality that all people and all ideologies have their strengths and weaknesses. We ignore the truth of the matter that at times we will be called upon to feel vulnerable, powerless, and afraid.

Projection

Projection is a defensive process in which our inner processes (thoughts, feelings, desires, etc.) are experienced as coming from the outer world rather than from within. It occurs when we attribute our own unacknowledged feelings to others. Projections often manifest as blame.

When we are engaging in projection, we might liken ourselves to a movie projector and others the screen upon which our inner processes are shone. Because we have projected our thoughts, feelings, desires, etc. outward and lost track of their origin, we now perceive others to be the ones who possess them. Sometimes this can seem dangerous to us, particularly if our own projected feelings are aggressive ones. Projection is the basis of paranoia.

Infants project because they experience themselves as the world and have not yet formed psychological boundaries between themselves and the world. Adults sometimes project for the same reason if they have little conscious sense of self. They also project to get rid of unwanted or hated parts of themselves. This is a relationship killer, as loved ones are terribly wounded and misunderstood when cast as having motives and qualities that are not actually present.

Introjection

Introjection is the opposite of projection and occurs when we experience what is coming from the outside as coming from the inside. It is a form of primitive identification with our significant others through which we instinctively take on their attitudes, qualities, and behaviors (usually those of Mommy or Daddy). Introjection is not a conscious decision to emulate those who are important to us so much as an unconscious process that occurs.

The unconscious identifications that introjection provides can be benign or quite dangerous. An example of a benign introjection/identification is when we take in the positive qualities of someone in our environment that we admire. An example of an introjection/identification that is somewhere in between healthy and destructive would be taking on the interests of another and thinking they are our own (a lack of development of our real interests). An example of destructive introjection/ identification would be identifying with an aggressor (hopefully to keep ourselves safe). Another is identifying so deeply with a loved one that, when they leave or die, we cannot get over our grief and depression because so much of them was taken in, internalized, and made part of our identity. In essence we have become them rather than ourselves. We are left depleted and empty without a real sense of self. So much of us is lost when our own development is ignored in favor of our deep attachment to and identification with another.

Splitting

Splitting is a method of separating parts of a whole in order to make sense of complex situations and elude the uncomfortable feelings that accompany them. It is used in children and adults alike. Children are very black and white in the way they see things. Their experiences are characterized as either good ones or bad ones; there is little in between. This inability to consider and integrate both polarities is a form of splitting. Splitting is a defense that adults also use quite handily to reduce their anxiety and maintain their self-esteem.

Splitting is used to make complex, confusing, or threatening situations seem less frightening. It is easier for us to split up things into right and wrong, good and evil, insiders and outsiders, right wing and left wing, etc. than it is for us to think and feel about all the intricacies of a situation. It is a way to order the world to be sure, but tends toward inflexibility, distortion, and absolutism.

Splitting becomes a serious personal problem when one starts splitting his or her own ego. This is an internal process that occurs when one aspect of self can be experienced but not its opposite. This leads to a poverty of self, a disconnection from others, and also disconnection from the self. It is terribly disruptive to relationships as it precludes the ability to have empathy (opposite views or qualities are experienced as foreign), it rules out acceptance of imperfect others (good or bad labels win out over a unified, overall assessment), and it predisposes one toward authoritarianism. Obviously, splitting results in distortion, as only parts of self or others are acknowledged.

Dissociation

Dissociation is similar to splitting. It comes into play when we isolate any of our mental processes from the rest of our psychic apparatus and this isolated mental process takes on independent functioning from the rest of us. [2] It is associated with out-of-body experiences or the "spaced out" feeling that we have when confronted with an extremely threatening situation. In severe cases it results in multiple personalities. It is used to cope when there is exposure to trauma that is overwhelming, painful, life threatening, or terrorizing (sexual abuse, war, violence, natural disasters, etc.). Dissociation temporarily does away with pain, dread, and horror, but leaves an array of intense emotions that must eventually be dealt with.

Now let's take a look at secondary defenses. The secondary defenses are:

Repression

Repression simply means motivated forgetting or ignoring. This is not the same thing as occasionally forgetting something that we will probably remember later. Rather, whatever it is that we have forgotten becomes consciously inaccessible due to its threatening nature. This forgotten memory has great power to distress us. We have no wish to visit it again. We have put it so far on the back burner that we have forgotten it is even there. This is common in post-traumatic stress disorder.

Regression

Regression means a return to an earlier, younger way of functioning. It can manifest as backsliding into childish, whiney, or needy behavior. Regression is an unconscious process. If we are consciously more needy than usual and seek comfort or reassurance, this does not qualify as regression.

Isolation

Isolation means separating a thought, idea, or memory from its emotional counterpart. Here we can think about something upsetting, but have no negative feelings about it. Or we can talk about something upsetting, but speak of it matter-of-factly as if it were insignificant. It usually results from traumatic emotional overstimulation.

In severe situations isolation can manifest as psychic numbing (prisoners of war, concentration camp survivors, survivors of natural disasters, etc.). This happens when we have anesthetized ourselves so fully that we feel nothing, yet those feelings living on within us cause havoc.

Aside from robbing us of our feelings and setting us up for future emotional problems, the use of isolation as a defense allows us to participate in situations that we would not have ordinarily chosen to participate in if we had allowed our feelings to be a factor. Without our feelings we can do all kinds of heinous things and not have the impact of our actions register. Isolation can block compassion.

The use of isolation can also cause us to move forward into situations that are potentially harmful to us. Through its use we effectively cut ourselves off from feeling the appropriate doubts and fears that would have been there if our emotions had been felt and considered.

Isolation is generally unconscious. A conscious version of it, however, can be valuable when trying to get something difficult done and to do it we have to stay emotionally uninvolved. For instance, doctors, therapists, judges, and soldiers have to employ this defense in order to do their jobs. If they got caught up in all the human suffering, nothing would ever get done. This, however, is a conscious, temporary coping strategy.

Intellectualization

Intellectualization is similar to isolation, but it is different in that it is used more to cope with everyday emotional overload than for traumatic overstimulation. Whereas with isolation we are not aware of having feelings, with intellectualization we know our feelings are there, but we refuse to experience them. Instead, we prefer to talk about them in a detached, intellectual manner. Due to this detachment, the emotional charge on our feelings does not get released. The use of this defense makes us appear cold, unfeeling, and robotic. It can result in very indifferent or hard-hearted behaviors. It also strongly inhibits emotional intimacy and closeness with others.

There are some people who actually celebrate their ability to always remain rational and non-emotional. The problem here is with the word *always*. Whereas it is a mature thing to be able to note our emotionally charged feelings and think about them rationally before we act, it is not healthy to consistently subordinate our feelings to intellect.

Rationalization

Rationalization is similar to intellectualization and refers to always having a reason for everything. Everything gets explained away and nothing is felt. For instance, if our spouses are rarely home, we can say the reason is that they are working hard. Yet we do not acknowledge how it feels not to have them at home much of the time. Or if something bad happens, we can say the reason is that it was put in our path to build our character or to give us a chance to burn off karma or learn from the experience. In reality, one or more of these things may be true, but none of them has anything to do with how the actual experience felt.

Rationalization oftentimes comes into play when we do not get something we want. Aside from giving ourselves a palatable reason for whatever has occurred, rationalization can help us convince ourselves that whatever we had wanted was actually not so desirable. For instance, perhaps our spouses are not home often enough, so we may try to rationalize that even if they were home, they would be too tired and cranky to enjoy anyway. Or we may not have been able to afford a house we wanted to but try to convince ourselves that it was too big for us regardless. All this is done in an effort to convince ourselves that when something bad happens, it is not so bad after all.

Rationalization can also be used to find and justify a particular pathway we wish to take. It is a method of convincing ourselves that this pathway is an acceptable one when in reality we may have emotional reservations regarding this route. For example, we may hit a child and convince ourselves that our display of aggression was for his or her own good. Or we may overcharge someone and rationalize that he or she is rich and can easily afford it. That way we do not have to acknowledge our greed and deceptiveness.

Moralization

Moralization is related to rationalization, but with a twist. With rationalization we are looking for a path to find ways to justify a reasonable direction we wish to take, but with moralization we are looking for a righteous reason to take that path. With the latter we feel that it is our duty to take this path. So rationalization takes what we already want to do and makes it okay in our minds; moralization justifies it and makes it a moral imperative. Not only is this defense irritating to many people with its inherent superiority, but its use can also justify all kinds of bad behavior as long as we can successfully convince ourselves that the behavior is in service of a very high purpose.

Compartmentalization

Compartmentalization occurs not when there is a separation between thought and feeling, but when there is a separation between two contradictory groups of thoughts. These two groups of thoughts can exist simultaneously without conscious confusion, conflict, shame, guilt, or anxiety. Compartmentalization can be best understood as a form of hypocrisy.

For example, there may be a person who is extremely religious yet steals; there may be a person who preaches marital faithfulness yet has affairs; there may be a person who believes in non-violence yet abuses his or her children; there may be a person who believes in inclusiveness yet is homophobic; there may be a person who believes in truthfulness yet lies.

Undoing

Undoing is the unconscious attempt to counterbalance an uncomfortable feeling with an attitude or behavior that will somehow eradicate it. Quite often this uncomfortable feeling is one of guilt or shame. When using this defense, we think that if we do something compensatory (like bring flowers to make up for our angry thoughts and/or behaviors), we can eradicate our guilt and shame and in the process wipe our slates clean. In this sense, undoing is similar to omnipotent control, i.e., the magical idea that through our own actions we can make almost anything appear or disappear. It is akin to superstition.

Undoing is not in play when we are bringing flowers home to make amends after we have erred if we have consciously observed our thoughts, feelings, and actions and are now honestly trying to make amends. Here our efforts are not to help ourselves feel better, but to truly care for another that we may have hurt.

Turning Against the Self/Self-Attack

Turning against the self, or self-attack, is a defense in which negative thoughts and feelings about another are redirected inwardly toward the self. We use it to safeguard ourselves by protecting others upon whom we depend, particularly when we are in a dependency situation and our well-being or lack of it depends on how that other person treats us. It is much easier to say "I'm stupid" or "It's all my fault" rather than direct a critical thought, feeling, or action toward an unsympathetic or moody caregiver. It is no picnic to acknowledge that our survival depends on a frightening, unstable, or undependable person. In fact, turning against the self is the basis for depression.

Despite the pain involved in believing that we are so flawed and culpable for pretty much everything, this defense gives us the illusion of having a sense of control over the situation. Anything is preferable to admitting that our very survival may be at stake and that we are powerless to change things. However, suffering through severe bouts of depression is difficult to survive as well, and many would say that the use of self-attack as a defense is not worth the pain.

Turning against the self is a secondary position rather than a primary one. The primary position is composed of whatever feelings are primarily present (perhaps fear, anger, sadness, or helplessness). The secondary position is a twisted, redirected version of these primary feelings that run more along the lines of guilt, shame, self-hate, worthlessness, and depression. We resort to the secondary position in an attempt to circumvent experiencing our primary feelings, but in actuality the secondary position is far more painful than the first as in the secondary position everything has been reframed as our loathsome fault.

Displacement

Displacement refers to the redirection of our thoughts, feelings, impulses, and behaviors to a secondary source rather than to the original source for which they were originally intended. This is done because there is too much anxiety associated with aiming our true thoughts, feelings, impulses, and behaviors in the original direction. This is the classic kicking the dog scenario. We are mad at our spouse, but this creates too much anxiety, so we kick the dog instead. Displacement is a factor in bullying, scapegoating, sexism, racism, and blaming. It is also in play when we are not angry with someone who has hurt or disappointed us in favor of being angry with others that we think contributed to the situation. An example of this would be when we are not angry with an unfaithful spouse, but with the "other" man or woman involved. Likewise, it is present when we are not upset with our own child's behavior in favor of being angry with those who influenced him or her.

Displacement can also come into play when we have unacceptable thoughts, feelings, and impulses that we redirect to more acceptable areas. For example, we may displace our sexual interest in someone's genitals to his or her feet, clothing, or footwear as in fetishes. Alternatively, we may divert our sexual interest for a forbidden person to an acceptable person. We may displace our rage with someone to ferociously cleaning the house. We may also divert anger or sadness into creative endeavors.

Reaction Formation

A reaction formation is a defense mechanism in which we turn one thing into its polar opposite in order to avoid experiencing our actual feelings. Usually it involves turning a negative feeling into a positive one; however, it can also involve turning a positive feeling into a negative one.

A classic example of a reaction formation that involves turning a negative feeling into a positive one occurs when a first child has to deal with negative feelings about a newborn child coming into the home. Feelings of competitiveness and jealousy are covered up with would-be feelings of love toward the baby or becoming mommy's little helper with the baby.

An example of turning a positive feeling such as attraction or longing into a negative one would be finally getting a date with an interesting person we really like and have wanted to go out with for a long time and then getting stood up. Rather than entertain our real feelings of disappointment, frustration, sadness, and anger, a reaction formation would have us say "I never wanted to go out with that jerk to begin with. I can't stand him or her!"

A reaction formation does not allow for ambivalence. It does not allow for the reality that we most likely have an array of feelings, both negative and positive, for a given individual or situation.

Reversal

Reversal is a defense in which we switch our role from subject to object or vice versa. For instance, if we have feelings of shame or fear about needing to be nurtured and cared for, we will place ourselves in a situation in which we can become a supportive caregiver. Here we are switching roles from being the object of nurturance to being the one who gives it and can vicariously identify with the other person's gratification in being nurtured. Similarly, we may be someone seeking psychotherapy who is uncomfortable in the role of patient and thus reverses roles by becoming overly inquisitive about our therapist's state of mind.

Another way to describe the defense of reversal is to say that we change our role from being that of the responder to that of the initiator. Or we might say that we change our role from being the *done to* to being the *doer*. This role reversal gives us the feeling of switching from powerlessness to powerfulness.

This defense is seen in sexual abuse survivors (the *done to*) who try to reverse their powerlessness by becoming promiscuous individuals who are now the ones who must give permission for sexual favors (the *doer*). It allows them to become the victimizers rather than the victims. It is also seen in individuals who are physically violent in an attempt to reverse the powerlessness of once having been subject to physical violence themselves.

Usually we seek to empower ourselves with this defense by changing our role to that of the *doer*; however, sometimes it is used to switch our role to that of the *done to*. For example, in masochistic individuals the defense of reversal can be used to redirect sadistic impulses that are initially aimed at others into sadistic impulses aimed at the self. This way masochistic individuals can be the ones who incur harm. In this manner they can retain the benefits of victimhood and perhaps surreptitiously express their sadism through inducing guilt in others. Alternatively, they may wish to stay in the victim position in order to expiate guilt and atone for imagined crimes.

Identification

Identification is similar to introjection in that it involves taking in another's qualities as our own, i.e., modeling ourselves after someone else. However, the defense of identification differs from that of introjection in that introjection is an unconscious occurrence and identification involves a conscious decision or at least partly conscious decision to identify with another.

Sometimes identification with others is benign and does not serve a defensive purpose. For instance, it is fine to want to be like someone who we value and respect. It is also fine to want to be skilled in some of the same areas as the person with whom we identify. There is no harm in any of this as long as we do not convince ourselves that we like something we do not or fail to develop our own interests. When we choose to cultivate qualities found in others, it is important that we avoid becoming someone other than ourselves.

It is not fine, however, to be like others because we fear them and need to align with them in order to avoid their hostility, i.e., identification with the aggressor. It is also not fine to take on their negative traits in order to abuse or intimidate others, thus giving ourselves an artificial power boost. Nor is it acceptable to be so aligned with others that, when they leave or die, we have nothing of us left. It is also not a good idea to rely on identification with others if we are suffering from a confusion of identity; it is better to find our own self.

Generally, anytime that modeling ourselves after another person is used as a defense to avoid painful feelings states, when it is used to build a self, or regain a sense of self-cohesion or self-esteem, it becomes a negative maneuver. Instead, we need to work through whatever is present emotionally rather than attempt to circumvent it by taking on others' characteristics.

Acting Out

Acting out is a defense that is characterized by the unconscious discharge of our thoughts, feelings, and impulses through action rather than through more mature avenues such as awareness, observation, reflection, talking, and delayed gratification. It only provides a temporary relief of inner tension and does not allow for any true mastery of our feelings. Acting out can involve overt motor behaviors (hitting, kicking, thrashing about, throwing things) as well as less obvious behaviors (verbal assaults, sexual impulsivity, exhibitionism, sadism, masochism, perversion). It is also present in all the compulsive behaviors (overeating, overshopping, overworking, over-partying, overdrinking, overdrugging, etc.). Acting out also encompasses all the unconscious behaviors we use to counter or supplant our acted-out behaviors such as counter-hostility, counter-compulsivity, counter-perversion, etc.

Individuals who rely on acting out behaviors to deal with the unacknowledged content of their inner world are said to be impulsive personalities.

Sexualization

Sexualization is a defense in which sexual activity and/or fantasy is unconsciously used to deal with unpleasant inner feeling states such as anxiety, low self-esteem, shame, boredom, envy, hostility, pain, or inner deadness. It is used to turn negative feeling states into feelings of excitement, power, and aliveness.

Sexual arousal is powerful and life-affirming. Consequently, all kinds of things are sexualized in order to obtain these feelings. A few things that are commonly sexualized are dependency (in females), aggression (in men), teachers/mentors, money, cars, clothing, hair, smoking, dirt, sweat, exercise, tool belts, food, and political status. Those in positions of power are routinely sexualized by persons in weaker positions, which allows the weaker individuals to avoid their feelings of envy, hostility, and fear of exploitation. Traumatic events that overwhelm a child's capacity to cope, such as abandonment, abuse, and invasive or painful medical procedures, can also be sexualized to turn a life-threatening event into a life-affirming one.

The macho man who maintains an aura of sexual potency is a classic example of an individual depending on a sexualized image in order to avoid feeling ordinary, fearful, powerless, envious, weak, unsure, ashamed, or low in self-esteem. In such individuals, eroticism is clearly a substitution of sexual power for actual personal power. The woman who eroticizes bad boys or abusive males in lieu of feeling her own fear, neediness, anger, powerlessness, or low self-esteem is yet another example of sexualization used for defensive purposes. This not only serves to diminish the woman's awareness of herself, but also can lead to a pattern of choosing men who are abusive to her.

Certainly, sexualization is not always a bad thing. We all have our fantasies, response patterns, and sexual preferences. However, attempting to convert our own pain into sexual excitement is not a healthy way to cope.

Sublimation

Sublimation refers to the channeling of our drives, impulses, and feelings into areas that are creative, interesting, healthy, and socially acceptable. Examples of this would be channeling our libidinal drive into artistic endeavors, directing our aggression into competitive sports, expressing our exhibitionism through the theater, or mentoring a niece or nephew if one cannot have a child of one's own. It has been said that while sublimation may not provide full satisfaction of a drive in quite the way we have envisioned, it can provide us with partial satisfaction or be surprisingly gratifying once we have found alternate pathways for expression. This defense has traditionally been considered to be somewhat healthy as it not only fosters socially acceptable behavior, but also allows for the discharge or partial discharge of our inner urges. It is still best, however, to have conscious knowledge of what drives us and choose our activities from that vantage point.

EMOTIONAL PROCESSING

Self-Attack

Chapter 9

UNDERSTANDING SELF-ATTACK

So far we have identified turning against the self or self-attack as one of our defenses. However, it is used so frequently and is responsible for so much suffering in this world that it has been given a section of its own in this book.

Self-attack as we will speak of it here is a harsh, unrelenting judgment held against the self that impedes emotional release and ultimately self-acceptance. This judgment results in deeply painful psychological states, typically taking the form of depression, guilt, shame, worthlessness, self-hatred, and self-recrimination. Feelings of rejection and hurt can also indicate self-attack. In its most severe form, it can manifest as suicide. In its lesser form, it can manifest as self-sabotage, procrastination, proneness to accidents, anxiety, addictions, perfectionism, and asceticism, to name a few.

Self-attack is very different from honestly assessing an aspect of our self that needs improvement and then making a move to remedy that. It is a vicious appraisal of the self that conveys an attitude of deep, personal failing. The self-attacking part of us is the terrorist element within us that decrees that we are bad, loathsome, incompetent, disposable, unimportant, and valueless. It reminds us how stupid and deficient we are, how contemptible we are, and how useless we are. It sadistically and consistently informs us that we are frauds, fools, and disappointments to all who know us. It makes sure that we know how eminently unlovable and easy to leave we really are.

Unfortunately, once the self-attacking part of us gets going, it tends to run on an endless loop within our heads. It works like a deeply embedded program that we just cannot seem to uninstall. The purpose of this section of the book is to help you learn how to beat the endless loop of self-hatred and get your inner terrorist under control.

While sometimes revealing itself on a conscious level, self-attack is generally an unconscious process. We can only know it is there by noticing all the tell-tale symptoms listed above. Sometimes we can also know it is present if we notice ourselves having self-deprecating fantasies. These are fantasies in which we are the ones who are hurt, abandoned, rejected, humiliated, or failing. We can also be tipped off to self-attack if we find ourselves going over lists of our crimes, replaying memories of hurtful situations, revisiting our failures, and reminding ourselves of our flaws.

The self-attack process starts with a redirection of our negative thoughts and feelings for others to our own self. Somehow we manage to effectively reroute our criticisms of others enough to turn everything into our own fault. The angrier we are with someone else, the more hateful we are to ourselves. Essentially, we are protecting them at our own expense.

Self-attack acts as a defense or barrier against our real feelings. Usually these feelings are aggressive feelings such as anger or rage, but they also include the authentic feelings that underlie our aggression such as sadness, fear, and helplessness. As such, self-attack prevents an awareness of what is emotionally going on within us. This, in turn, prevents a healthy working-through of those unacknowledged feelings. Once this lack of awareness and lack of emotional movement is in play, there is little hope of getting past the skin-crawling feeling of self-hatred.

Because self-attack acts as a defense against feeling, it can be said that it does not represent a primary position. It represents a secondary position. It is there only to keep our true primary feelings out of our awareness, to keep them from being heard, and to prevent them from releasing. Even though only a secondary position, self-attack does a very effective job of eradicating all knowledge of our primary feelings. In their place, however, it leaves a horrific legacy.

The problem here is that the secondary feelings brought on by self-attack are so painful, so self-deprecating, and so loathsome that one has to wonder if our primary feelings could be much worse. As it turns out, our primary feelings are far less painful than those brought by self-attack. We are simply too afraid of our primary feelings to experience them and work them through. This sounds strange, yet it is true. We are terrified of our real feelings for fear of losing control, of going crazy, of getting depressed, of acting inappropriately, of being in too much pain, to name a few of our worries. Yet in reality all those things occur from being stuck in an endless spiral of self-attack, not from processing our primary feelings.

It is important to understand that feelings of self-attack cannot be moved and thereby released. Only the primary feelings can be moved. This is because self-attack is usually composed of a variety of feelings that cannot be individually identified and worked through. It is a package deal. A package deal cannot be released. The feelings must be dealt with individually.

Self-attack is also difficult to release because the emotional self is very afraid of judgment from the rational self and the superego/ conscience. It would rather be in the pain of self-loathing than experience the non-acceptance of its primary feelings. It wants to be heard and understood.

In addition, self-attack can be difficult to release due to the fact that it can involve protecting highly valued individuals in our lives. These are people who we may deeply love and/or depend upon. In such cases we protect them from our feelings at our own expense so that we do not have to face the pain of their a reactions, judgments, and/or abandonment. Our dread of loss is too great.

Whether judgment and non-acceptance come from within or without, it is a huge deterrent to the release of self-attack. While we do not control the responses of those in the external world, luckily we can learn to control our inner judgments and to cultivate an inner environment of compassion and acceptance. At least then we have a fighting chance of unloading the nasty pronouncements that we direct against ourselves.

Chapter 10

OBSERVING THE PRESENCE OF
SELF-ATTACK

As we move on to observing the presence of self-attack, there will be a slight change in the way that we characterize it. So far, we have portrayed it as a defense mechanism that we sometimes use against ourselves. This is correct. However, in this chapter we will portray our self-attacking mechanism as a separate entity. Specifically, we will call it our *inner self-attacker*.

In the same way that we sometimes separate and then personify our emotional self by seeing it as an inner child or the way that we separate and personify our rational self by seeing it as our inner intellectual, we need to separate and personify our self-attack. This is simply a process of distinguishing one part of self from another and then personalizing it so that it is easier to interact with. This will help us to better observe and deter our self-attacking element.

Self-observation is vital to the process of gaining mastery over our self-attacking process. Without it our inner self-attacker runs free under the cloak of darkness, able to wreak havoc at will. In order to disarm this attacker, we first need to observe the tell-tale feelings, symptoms, and behaviors indicating the presence of self-attack (depression, guilt, shame/humiliation, self-deprecation/self-blame, lack of self-forgiveness, high anxiety, low self-esteem, accident proneness, perfectionism, psychosomatic illnesses, self-sabotage, etc.). In doing so we can acknowledge the vicious, condemnatory process that is in play. Secondly, we need to challenge our inner self-attacker. The minute we observe it, we must strongly and unilaterally dispute its validity. This allows us to divert our attention away from the false, denigrating pronouncements of our inner self-attacker and place our attention on our primary feelings that are waiting to be processed.

Sometimes it can be helpful to see the inner self-attacker as a villain that we know from a movie or television show. It is best to choose someone who we experience to be truly dastardly rather than someone we experience as funny. Once this is done, the process of observing and challenging can move ahead.

At first this villainous figure will appear to be very powerful, and we might feel profoundly afraid of him/her. In fact, it may seem almost impossible to challenge such a formidable character, much less in a strong, unilateral manner. If we do find ourselves unable to challenge our inner self-attacker, we should not force our self to do so. We should just observe our opponent, perhaps from behind the safety of a wall or from behind a bush. Just watch. That is all. After many, many observations — maybe even hundreds — our inner self-attacker's presence will seem to diminish and a challenge can be made. Sometimes the challenge will merely be a stepping out from behind the wall and letting our own powerful presence be known. Sometimes it will be a swift kick in the inner self-attacker's posterior end. Sometimes it will be a dismissive glance before proceeding with our own acts of self-care.

A new challenge should be issued each time our inner self-attacker makes his/her presence known, because self-attack is always invalid and invariably lets us know that we are on the wrong path. In fact, it is so far afield from correct emotional processing that an immediate challenge should become an automatic response no matter how worthless, unlovable, and insignificant we may feel. Our inner self-attacker should not be afforded any chance at all. Its only value is that it shows us how off base we are and how much we need to attend to the primary feelings that were present before we succumbed to self-attack.

After a challenge has been issued, we can move on to determine what our primary feelings are and minister to them whenever we want. We can start seeing how statements like "I must be easy to leave" or "I'm such a fool to have ever trusted him/her" or "He/she never loved me to begin with" actually indicate feelings of shock, disillusionment, rage, disgust, emptiness, loneliness, and grief. These are the feelings we should be processing, not giving credence to our inner self-attacker's phony pronouncements that we are worthless, disposable, foolish, and unlovable.

If we find that we are so hypnotized by our inner self-attacker's accusations that we cannot challenge him/her, nor can we move on to processing our real feelings, we can at least continue to observe our nemesis. Observing our inner self-attacker's unholy presence can be quite a self-attack-busting move in itself. Why is this? Strangely, the act of observation in itself diminishes whatever difficulty is being observed. It is a similar dynamic to calling someone out and not letting their actions go unnoticed. Even if we do not implement any of the other tools at our disposal, steady, consistent observation will weaken our inner self-attacker and keep us clear on the fact that we stand separate from him/her.

A simple rule of thumb here is that *when we become aware of the fact that we are attacking ourselves, i.e., feeling depressed, rejected, stupid, expendable, ashamed, guilty, worthless, etc., we must immediately acknowledge that we are off base. In fact, we are supremely off base.* Acknowledging this fact alone can keep us from fully succumbing to our inner self-attacker. In instances where, despite our best efforts, we cannot shake off our depressive or self-recriminating convictions, we need to hang on to this rule. It will help us remain focused on the truth. It changes the focus from the certainty that we are worthless to the certainty that we are worthwhile, but simply cannot feel it at this moment. It can help us observe the reality that, while engaged in self-attack, we are engaged in a bogus activity; we are in the middle of a twisted psychological process; our perceptions are off; our coping mechanism has temporarily gone haywire; our brain chemistry is out of balance. This is very different from believing what we are feeling while engaging in a terrorist attack on the self. At no time should we forget the rule. Again, *at no time should we forget the rule.*

Chapter 11

FINDING THE PRIMARY FEELINGS THAT UNDERLIE SELF-ATTACK

In this chapter we will look at several areas of self-attack and the four primary feelings that underlie them. We will also take a look at how our superego/conscience sets us up for self-attack. Let's start with guilt.

Guilt typically occurs when we violate an ethical, moral, social, or religious code. It also occurs when we indulge in supposedly unacceptable thoughts or feelings. These violations create an inner conflict between right and wrong and often lead to self-punishment. The part of us that determines whether or not we are in need of punishment is called the superego or conscience. The superego/conscience is a collection of ethical and moral principles that are meant to deter certain feelings, thoughts, intentions, and behaviors. It is instilled by our parents or other significant individuals and reflects their personal values as well as their stringency or lack of it. Thus, the conscience is constructed; it is not inherent. Nor is it associated with our intuition or inner guidance system.

The superego/conscience has several mechanisms with which to activate self-attack. One of its favorites, however, is guilt induction. Guilt punishes us by creating a loss of self-esteem. It would have us believe that we are bad individuals for daring to violate certain standards of behavior, thought, and/or feeling. If we agree with these standards, we need to forgive ourselves for our transgressions. If we do not agree with them, we need to validate ourselves and follow our own paths. Yet if we do follow our own paths, oftentimes our guilt chastises us and creates doubt that our choices have any validity at all. It undermines our confidence and destroys our self-regard. Guilt leaves little room for inner truth. In addition, it fails to leave room for empathy or understanding regarding our human frailties and struggles.

Although there is a variety of primary feelings that can reside beneath our guilt, there are four primary feelings that occur most often. These are feelings of anger, fear, sadness, and helplessness. When identified and experienced, any of these primary feelings is far less painful than the depressive, guilt-ridden, or shame-based feelings brought on by self-attack. Because experiencing our primary feelings can be so restorative, it is important that we learn more about their role in mitigating self-attack. It is also important that we learn to identify them as quickly as possible.

Consider the following example. Envision yourself to be a 25-year-old adult who, for financial reasons, has had to move back home with Mom and Dad. Your parents still see you as a child and treat you accordingly. One of the things they do is to strictly enforce an unreasonable curfew. They will not budge on this rule. Your father is a bear, and your mother passively acquiesces to him. Now you find yourself tip-toeing into their house a full two hours past curfew. You feel terribly guilty. After all, they are trying to help you out during a difficult time. The least you can do is follow their rules. Your guilt feelings are excruciating.

If you were to take a look at your primary feelings, you might find the following:

- Before you went straight to the self-attacking position of guilt, you were feeling anger. "Why do Mom and Dad have to be so unreasonable? Who do they think they are? Why are they enforcing such adolescent boundaries on an adult? Is anyone ever allowed to grow up and individuate in this family? Why can't they understand that everyone needs to get out and let loose a bit?"

You were also angry to be in this dependent position to begin with. You didn't go to college just to lose your job and not be able to find a new one.

- Before you went straight to the self-attacking position of guilt, you were feeling fear —lots and lots of fear. "What is going to happen now? Will there be a terrible fight? Will I be asked to leave? If so, where will I go? Will I now be seen as a disappointment? Will there be a loss of love or esteem? Will Mom have to put up with Dad's foul mood for days because of my actions? Will my actions be broadcast to other family members and portrayed in a bad light? Will there be recriminations about my financial reversal? Will I be touted as a deadbeat even though I am doing all I can to find a job?"

- Before you went straight to the self-attacking position of guilt, you were feeling sadness. You had deep sadness over having studied so long and tried so hard only to lose your job and end up back home. You were sad that you have to reinvent yourself when you thought your path was set. You were also sad that your mother and father have had to go out of their way to help you when they have already helped so much throughout your life. You were sad that some of your dreams about finding success in life if you follow all the rules have been shattered. You were sad that you feel diminished and dependent. You were sad that life is so difficult.

- Before you went straight to the self-attacking position of guilt, you were feeling helpless. You were helpless to do any more at this time to better your situation despite all your efforts. You were helpless to make time go any faster. You were helpless to forge your own path without depending on others and without draining their resources. You felt helpless that you tried so hard and still could not succeed. You felt helpless in the face of bad things happening to good people.

If you allow yourself to feel these primary feelings in a non-judgmental, understanding manner, you may feel like a frightened person, an angry person, a sad person, or a helpless person, but you will not feel like a culpable person, a defective person, or a bad person. It is feeling culpable, defective, or a bad that is the problem. Not one of the four primary feelings listed above could ever, ever be as difficult or painful to deal with as any of these feelings.

Even when you legitimately think that, yes indeed, you are in the wrong and you have behaved inappropriately, the healthy feelings to have would be feelings of sadness, humility, and regret. These feelings might be followed by a sincere action to correct the situation. Your feelings should not be the self-hating feelings of being blameworthy, deficient, immoral, or bad.

A second area of self-attack that we need to familiarize ourselves with is that of depression. Depression is created by turning anger against the self. Here we have decided that a particular problem must be our fault rather than someone else's. It involves tremendous self-blame and self-vilification rather than letting ourselves know with whom or with what we are actually angry. Sometimes we are angry with a specific person, sometimes with the general loss of control in our lives, sometimes with the degree of suffering we are called upon to experience, and sometimes with the feeling of being forsaken by everyone.

Behind that anger is usually deep grief. This grief, however, is not allowed to move. It is being held still by our self-attack. Consequently, our grief is denied a hearing. Most of us think that depression is grief. It is not. It is a diversion from grief. It is a painful, self-hating blame-state that completely denies healthy grieving.

Behind our anger and grief, we often carry a great deal of fear. We may be absolutely terrorized about our situation, yet only experience ourselves to be depressed individuals who simply cannot cope. This is just one more thing to hold against ourselves. After all, our inner self-attacker has convinced us that everything is our fault.

The same thing holds true for helplessness and powerlessness. When depressed, we simply cannot access our personal power. What power? We feel like we are useless, with nothing to offer and no ability to make anything different.

Consider this example: Let's say that you are feeling very depressed, particularly over your love life. You have just gotten dumped by a complete jerk. You cannot believe that you could have ever chosen such an incredibly bad partner. You are judging your ability to be discerning and to make good choices. You are judging how long you stayed in the relationship. You are judging being needy. You feel foolish, humiliated, devalued, and disposable. You feel worthless — like a used tissue that was so easy to throw away.

All of this is, of course, self-attacking trash talk. In such a situation you need to admit that:

- You are enraged and want to hurt the person who has deserted you as much as he or she has hurt you. You are enraged that for all the effort put forth, you were never really known, heard, or understood. You are enraged that so much time and effort has been completely wasted. You are enraged over the untruths and misperceptions that abound. You are enraged that somehow the perpetrator seems to be getting off scot free. You are enraged that he or she does not seem to be hurting the way you are. You are enraged that the perpetrator can move on so easily after all the damage that has been done. You are enraged that he or she has taken no responsibility in the matter at all and sees himself or herself as blameless. You are enraged that you have been exploited and used up.

- You fear your loneliness. You are afraid that you are not loveable. You fear your own need. You fear not having support. You fear the depth of your sorrow. You fear becoming so jaded that you will not trust again. You fear the untruths that may be told about you with no way to set the record straight. You fear being deeply misunderstood. You fear that secretly you are a bad person.

- You are sad and disappointed that so much effort could come to naught. You are sad over mistakes made. You are shocked and saddened by the fact that you were never known for who you really you are. You are deeply saddened that someone as valuable as you could be beaten so badly. You are sad that you ever exposed yourself to such a person. You are sad that you did not have enough information or experience to know how to be successful in this relationship. You feel sad that you are lonely and unsupported. You feel sad that you do not feel special and wanted anymore. You feel sad that you feel empty.

- You feel helpless to ever get through to this person. You feel helpless to change his or her perceptions or way of handling problems. You feel powerless to succeed in the face of his or her unresolved historical problems or mental health problems. You feel helpless to easily get past your grief without having to suffer terribly. You feel helpless to ever get this individual to see and to register what he or she has done.

Third, let's take a look at the role of self-attack in the creation of shame. Shame is directly related to self-attack. It is yet another way that our misdirected anger manages to discredit, dishonor, and disgrace us. Shame is a particularly vicious form of self-attack because it is based on the conviction that there is something fundamentally flawed about us. Here we do not just see ourselves as stupid, foolish, unworthy, bad, or failing in a given setting. We see ourselves as loathsome and incompetent to the core. We are easily humiliated and carry a deep sense of embarrassment about who we are. Shame can be difficult to offload. Nevertheless, we will find relief if we can get in touch with the primary feelings that underlie our shame.

Consider this example: You have studied for years to be a lawyer. You are the first person in your family to go to college, much less get an advanced degree. You have always made good grades. You have been chosen for many honors. Now everyone is expecting a lot from you.

Your family's honor seems to depend upon your success. You feel pressured to do well because of their need for validation and because, historically, being successful has been your only way to get love. You already have a good job lined up upon passing the bar. It is at a big, upscale law firm. You take the bar and fail. You lose your chance at that job. Your family is hysterical and hypercritical. You feel deeply ashamed.

If you take a look at the primary feelings that underlie your shame, you might find the following:

- "I am afraid that I will never be loved for myself. I am afraid that I will never succeed. I am afraid that people are laughing at me. I am afraid to try again for fear of exposure. I am afraid of the depth of my loneliness if I have to hide my whole life so as not to be exposed. I am afraid to tell off the people who attempt to shame me. I am afraid to tell my family that sometimes they hinder more than help."

- "I am angry that others are as judgmental and insensitive as they are. I am angry that I was given so little support in my formative years that this is what I now struggle with. I am angry that I am afraid as much as I am. I am angry with the concept of perfectionism. Nobody is perfect and there should be room for imperfection in this world. I am also angry that my family's honor seems to depend on me. This makes me feel used. Let them get their own honor."

- "I am sad that I hate myself so much. I am sad that I put so much pressure on myself. I am sad that I have to struggle with so much fear. I am sad that life is not any easier than it is. I am sad that I feel so weak. I am sad that I have never been praised or validated except by being successful."

- "I am helpless to alter others' opinions of me. I am helpless to change my upbringing, although I am not helpless to change my future."

All of these primary feelings keep self-loathing at bay and impart an enhanced sense of empathy for our life struggles. They help us to see ourselves as good people who may be flawed, but are endeavoring to do the very best that we can.

Chapter 12

CIRCUMVENTING JUDGMENT OF PRIMARY FEELINGS

The secret to circumventing self-attack is to allow the primary feelings that we uncover to be whatever they are without judgment. These feelings desperately need understanding and acceptance, but rarely do they get it. Instead, they get judgment. When our feelings receive judgment, they cannot find release. Consequently, they stay attached to the judgment and continue to empower it.

Judgment is an evaluative, mental process. It separates good from bad, acceptable from unacceptable, useful from useless. In its positive sense, it uses its ability to help us find clarity and choose constructive pathways. However, in its negative sense it can be harshly evaluative and condemnatory. The latter offers only conditional love, saying in essence that we are acceptable only if we agree that things are the way our judgmental, rational self says they are. [1] When dealing with self-attack, we certainly do not need this. Instead, we need to give our primary feelings unconditional love, which accepts things the way they are.

When we find ourselves judging our feelings, this usually means that we have bypassed our visceral experience of an emotion and have instead gone into our heads. We have abandoned the real awareness and real experience of our feelings and moved our attention up into our mental processes where we have replaced something real with thoughts about something real. At the very least, this can prematurely take us away from an identification and experience of our feelings. At worst, those thoughts can be used to further our self-hate.

When we notice ourselves adversely judging our self, it is important to immediately stop the judgment process and go back to whatever we were originally feeling. If we are able to successfully get out of our heads and back in touch with the original feeling so we can meet that feeling with understanding and acceptance, we can quickly subvert another round of self-attack.

Judgment is very unyielding as it presupposes that we are unable to change an offending behavior or alter an unacceptable situation. It exists out of time and so remains in place long after we have changed a behavior or altered a bad situation. [2] Because of this, no matter how much we change, we are stuck with the bound-up emotional energy that our judgments hold in place. Until the primary feelings underlying our judgments are heard and accepted, the judgments will remain. In fact, each time a judgment is revisited, the feelings behind that judgment remain unmoved or they are intensified, and release of them becomes more difficult.[3]

Judgment has its place. There are all sorts of things that need to be carefully sorted out and evaluated. Judgment against our deepest and truest emotions, however, is not one of those things. Certainly, we can assess what is working in our lives and what is not, thereby coming up with behavioral or life-style changes that will help our emotional self feel better, but we cannot hand down harsh value judgments and expect to feel peace.

Instead, we should always strive to understand how we might feel as we do, particularly if we have a difficult history that affects us deeply. In such cases we are already emotionally bruised and battered, leaving us with a limited ability to take much more abuse.

We must also come to a firm realization of the fact that on this plane of existence, we are human beings with human-proportioned selves — not gods with godlike proportions. We are limited in our earthly capacities, and we are far from perfect. As humans, we struggle mightily with our life experiences and the growth that they bring. Judgements surrounding them abound. However, despite our limitations and imperfections, our life experiences are the only way to learn about ourselves and to evolve in our consciousness.

Because we cannot evolve in our consciousness without individuated life experience and all the awareness that it brings, we should avoid wasting the opportunities afforded us in this lifetime by trying to be saints. While we can aspire to be loving and compassionate people, we need to refrain from demanding super-human, transcendent perfection from ourselves. That would be like expecting a two-year-old to have the cognition and motor skills of an adult.

What makes our actual feelings seem so deeply unacceptable? Sometimes it is because we tell ourselves that our feelings are childish or infantile. We deem them to be not at all mature and reasonable. We do not like the prospect of immature functioning, nor do we think others will. We therefore demand feelings from ourselves that reflect perfect development and maturation.

Unfortunately, there is no such thing as perfect development and maturation. We are all flawed in some way. When our primary feelings seem immature, we need to let them be just that. We should not attempt to renovate them at all. After all, in the end, after consideration of all things, we are probably not going to act on them.

Rather than try to renovate our immature side, we should strive to understand that our feelings come from the part of the brain that is reactive. Its whole job is to react to sensation. It cannot do anything else other than to produce gut level responses. This part of the brain will always be a child and react like a child. It is best to acknowledge its limited capabilities and accept its emotional truth rather than try to make it be an adult. There are other parts of our brain that will help us make constructive decisions.

One of the biggest things we judge ourselves for is our need. It is important to remember that until we are somewhat advanced in our knowledge of self, we can only choose within the context of our own need. We all have need — sometimes a lot of it. At times it is worse than others. Need makes us feel weak and vulnerable. It embarrasses us. It alters our decisions. We fear it. Whatever the case, we have to befriend it and let it be known in its nakedness.

We are needy for very good reasons. Perhaps a certain need of ours was not met sufficiently in our youth or we have not yet achieved enough individuation or independence to know our own capabilities. Maybe we are unusually lonely, we have endured sustained stress, we have suffered the loss of someone we depended on, we have been emotionally beaten up, we have over-given, or we are thoroughly exhausted. Perhaps we are simply young and our self-reliance is still to come. Perhaps we are inducing feelings of neediness from those around us; feelings are very contagious. The list could go on. The point is that need is present for a reason. Need, in particular, should be embraced and deeply understood.

Another thing that makes our feelings seem so deeply unacceptable is that when we are hurt, sad, vulnerable, or disillusioned, we tell ourselves we should have chosen our partner, job, friend, etc. more judiciously. We say that we should have known better. We can hardly believe that we overlooked the obvious warning signs.

Sometimes it is true that we know ahead of time that something will not be good for us and still plunge straight ahead. Yet most of the time we do this due to an unfulfilled emotional need that we are desperately trying to fulfill. Oftentimes we are trying to fill our emptiness. We may be trying to escape terrible emotional pain that we carry and are attempting to get back to emotional equilibrium. These things drive us to overlook the realities of this world and the consequences of our actions. Intellect seldom trumps emotional need or pain.

At times we think we know something ahead of time when in reality we do not know all the variables. In fact, we are woefully naïve, uninformed, and inexperienced about the matter at hand. In some cases, we cannot possibly know what is going on because we have lived in a dysfunctional situation for so long that it feels normal. We may tell ourselves that we know what we are doing and may even feel like we know what we are doing, but in actuality our knowledge is limited. Teenagers are famous for this. In reality we can only choose according to the information that we have at the time. We cannot know what we do not know. We do not exist as a combination of psychologist, professor, doctor, lawyer, sociologist, mechanic, and psychic. We have to learn to be okay with not knowing everything.

Occasionally we find our real feelings to be unacceptable because our bad choices seem repetitive and self-sabotaging. Sadly, before we come to know ourselves, we can only choose within the context of our own personal issues and our own internal programming. These two factors have a massive impact on our choices. Many times they drive our behaviors blindly. This is why we should all embark on the process of self-discovery. It is a beautiful and enlightening journey. We can overcome many of our problems and become wonderfully cognizant of our conditioning by working on our personal growth, but we cannot achieve mastery of every single thing within us. We can only make choices based on our level of self-awareness at any given point in time.

Every now and then we have difficulty accepting and understanding our real feelings because our guilt is saying things like "But you're not a child. You're an adult. Act like one." Or it is saying things like "If you were a good mother/father/wife/ husband, you would feel more forgiving. If you were a good person, you would give everyone a chance and you would include them no matter how you feel about them. If you were a good person, you would feel like giving to others. If you were a good person, you would never feel sadistic, punitive, or full of hate."

These ridiculous mandates about how terrible we are if we feel whatever we actually feel are tremendously destructive. They keep the self-hating cycle going endlessly. Do not buy into them! For all we know, our feelings may be transient ones that, given a chance to be heard, would dissipate almost immediately. They would release precisely because they were allowed to vibrate and to move. This is what we want — movement — not some rigid morality that lets absolutely nothing within us shift.

If this idea of giving emotions room to move is frightening, remember that we are just doing the work of releasing emotion here. We will not be automatically basing our behaviors on the emotions we are striving to release. After rational thought (sans harsh judgment) has been introduced, we may or may not base our actions on our primary feelings. However, we should not allow thought to interfere with the initial process of welcoming and understanding them.

It should always be remembered that guilt is part of our self-attacking mechanism. Its doubt-inducing pronouncements never come from a valid place. Some say that there is appropriate guilt and inappropriate guilt. This is an interesting point that has some validity. However, if we regret something that we have done, feel terrible about it, and have made amends, it is still preferable to allow ourselves an experience of our primary feelings rather than allow self-attack as a response. We can feel deep regret and rectify our actions without hating ourselves endlessly.

Chapter 13

USING OUR THOUGHT PROCESSES TO LESSEN SELF-ATTACK

In Chapter 6 a variety of thought processes were discussed in the general sense. Among them were perceptions, beliefs, and expectations. In this chapter we will look at these three thought processes as they can be used specifically to reduce self-attack. Let's start with perceptions, i.e., the way we interpret our environment.

Eighty percent of our stress is caused not by events that occur within our lives, but by our interpretation of those events. So it is with self-attack. Many of our self-deprecating feelings and convictions are the end result of incorrect perception of our life events.

Each time a life-event occurs, we automatically do a mini-evaluation of it. We look for a way to see it, to frame it, and to understand it. We immediately look for an explanation of why it occurred. Another way to say this is that we tell ourselves a little story about what just happened. Usually all of this occurs out of our consciousness and in a split second.

Unfortunately, the stories we tell ourselves are usually far from accurate. This is because the life event in question is quickly run through all of the memory-laden filters that exist within us. These may be filters from our upbringing, from all of our life experiences to date, or ones we have single-handedly manufactured from our own fears and self-condemnations. Wherever they originate, they can skew our perceptions, causing us to interpret benign, current-day events in a dismal, hurtful, self-attacking manner.

Here is an example of how it works. Say someone we care about cancels plans with us that we were looking forward to. We immediately start devising a storyline to explain why this occurred. We can either tell ourselves that the cancellation happened because we are unwanted and unimportant or because there may have been conflicting plans or extenuating circumstances. One story is going to be more along the lines of truth and the other a bad fairy tale. We need to choose. To do this we have to determine which story was the result of one of our self-attacking filters. The correct story will not leave us feeling worthless, rejected, and hurt. It will only leave us feeling disappointed or sad, and possibly resigned. Even if the true story turns out to be that the other person is less interested in us than we are in him or her, this is still unrelated to our worth or lovability. As the expression goes, it's just one of those things.

Sadly, we all hold a number of self-attack filters through which we view incoming information. Two that are very common are our expectation-of-rejection filter and our conviction-of-worthlessness filter. A few related filters are our conviction-that-we-are-unlovable filter, our conviction-that-we-are-disposable filter, our conviction-that-we-were-never-really-loved-to-begin-with filter, our expectation-of-failure filter, our expectation-of-being-used-and-taken-advantage-of filter, and our conviction-that-we-are-stupid-for-trusting filter. All are extremely damaging and should be avoided at all cost.

It is best that we note this process of mental interpretation and consciously start to observe how we are deciphering our life events. If we notice that we are automatically interpreting our life experiences in a self-attacking manner, it then becomes our duty to try out a new interpretation. Ultimately we are free to choose which one we will settle on, but hopefully it will be a less self-deprecating one. Thus we have started the process of replacing unconsciousness with consciousness and non-reality with reality. This is a self-attack-busting duo.

A second way to lessen self-attack through our thought processes is to examine the thoughts/beliefs that we hold and note the way that they alter our feelings. Some of these might sound like "I believe . . .

- I need to be perfect."
- I need to have a thin/curvy body."
- I should always be productive."
- I should always do the best I can."
- I should always remain strong and in control."
- I am not very smart."
- there is only one right way to do things."
- once committed, I should never change my mind."
- I should always be kind, thoughtful, and altruistic no matter how exhausted I am."

It is true that sometimes we feel however we feel, and a new belief cannot easily turn the tide. Self-attack can be very stubborn and resistant that way. Certainly we cannot just pull a new belief out of a hat and everything will come up roses. But we do at least need to attempt to make a change in the way we think about life and the things we demand of ourselves. The list of *shoulds* that we hold up for ourselves as a standard is both daunting and unrealistic. We need to give ourselves a break. We need to dare to be human.

Yet another way we can mentally help ourselves overcome self-attack is to pay attention to the rigidity of our belief system. Sometimes we get going with a well-intentioned belief that, taken too far, loses its validity. Actually pretty much any belief taken too far loses its validity. We need to see where a valid belief turns into an invalid one. Consider the belief that we should always be accepting of others. This is just fine until we come upon a person who intends to harm us, manipulate us, or drain us. In such a situation we should not rely on our belief so much as our intuition and intention to promote self-care.

The minute we assess that a rigid belief no longer applies, we can expect a big reaction from our inner self-attacker who will bombard us with recriminations. Its attempt to punish us for daring to reconsider the present validity of our belief will be swift and hard. Yet if we understand that our beliefs must be tempered by the needs of the present moment, and that they are present to serve us and not the other way around, we can meet our inner self-attacker with a firm hand.

A third thing we can do to lessen self-attack is to examine the nature and scope of our expectations. If we are not to be consistently disappointed and self-attacking, our expectations need to be realistic and somewhat mature. They cannot be unrealistic and over-inflated. Nor can they reflect all of our childhood dreams and longings. If they do, we will be consistently and bitterly disappointed.

Moreover, if we are not to be in a constant state of disillusionment and self-loathing, our expectations need to be more like preferences rather than unyielding demands for specific outcomes. Of course there are some expectations that we cannot compromise on, such as the expectation that we be treated with consideration and respect. However, many of our expectations should have a little wiggle room. Our entire sense of self-esteem and well-being should not depend on whether or not someone lived up to our expectations. The act of changing expectations to preferences is a potent tool in our efforts to accept reality and to be at peace.

We can err in either the direction of having expectations that are too high or the direction of having them be too low. Expectations that are too high put a huge burden on those around us and place us in the fragile position of needing them to be filled in order to be okay. Expectations that are too low allow others to harm us or run all over us with impunity. Such expectations invite victimization and reinforce our unworthiness. They also set us up to over-function for others and under-function for ourselves, i.e., we end up doing everything for everyone else and doing very little for ourselves.

If we can keep our expectations modulated, suited to the constraints of the present moment, and in the preference zone rather than the demand zone, we will find our level of self-attack greatly diminish. Otherwise, we will have set everyone in our environment up to fail and set ourselves up to feel repeatedly undervalued and unfulfilled.

Chapter 14

SELF-TALK

After we have observed how our faulty thought processes are contributing to self-attack, we need to go a step further and become aware of the negative self-talk that they are generating. In other words, we need to pay attention to the way we are talking to ourselves based on our misperceptions of the environment, our denigrating thoughts, our rigid belief systems, and our outlandish expectations.

At first glance, faulty thought processes and negative self-talk seem like the same thing; however, they are a bit different from each other. The major distinction between the two is that self-talk is a more active factor in self-attack than are faulty thought processes. Self-talk builds upon our incorrect ways of looking at the world and involves active, ongoing, incorrect information being fed to the emotional self.

When we observe an error in our thought processes, we then need to then listen carefully to the self-talk that follows. We need to hear how we sound when we talk to our emotional self. Are we supporting the inaccuracy in our thought processes by speaking to our emotional self in disparaging, cruel, frightening ways or are we correcting the error by speaking to our emotional self in kind, encouraging, comforting ways? If we have any kind of depression, anxiety, guilt, shame, self-recrimination, self-loathing, or rejection going on, we are definitely engaging in the former.

In these cases we are probably saying things like . . .

- You're stupid.
- You're worthless.
- You're unlovable.
- No one wants you.
- You're a fool.
- You were never loved to begin with.
- You're weak.
- Don't even bother to try.
- You're a failure.
- You're no good.
- Your feelings don't count.
- This is just your lot in life.
- You might as well give up.
- You're not good looking.
- No one will ever choose you.
- You're going to be alone forever.
- You're in great danger.
- You have no choices.
- You might starve.
- You'll probably die.

When speaking to our emotional self, it can be very helpful to personify it, thereby seeing it as separate entity. It is especially effective to see it as a young child who is in need of our care. This makes what we are inwardly saying seem more real and makes us realize how exceptionally cruel we are in being able to attack a child. It is particularly shocking to see that we are capable of doing this to our own vulnerable, trusting, inner child — the same child that has given us its emotional support throughout our lifetime.

Even though we may envision ourselves as kind, loving individuals, we need to honestly take note of how viciously we speak to ourselves. We need to familiarize ourselves with our aggressive drive — what it feels like, what it sounds like, and how it expresses itself through our behaviors. Typically, it will be critical, sarcastic, impatient, demanding, withholding, unforgiving, mean, hateful, sadistic, violent, and/or downright murderous. It loves punishment and revenge. It can be gleeful and satisfied in the face of another's misfortune. It can express itself directly out in the open or passively under the cloak of innocence. Our aggressive drive is appropriate when facing danger or defending ourselves, but it is not appropriate in dealing with our inner child.

Assuming that we can keep our aggressive drive in check, it can be very helpful to have opportune conversations with the emotional self. If we are anxious, these conversations should be soothing, encouraging, and reassuring. They can also be conversations that bring new, salient information. Perhaps we will present a plan of action to the emotional self that will help matters. At the very least, we will show it that we are working diligently to figure things out. We might let it know that we are a team. Perhaps we will simply remind the emotional self of that which we do not control and refocus it on what can be controlled. Similarly, we may refocus it on all of our blessings.

When dealing with anxiety and/or depression, under no circumstances should we give ourselves frightening, dismal, predictive messages about our prospects for survival. We can acknowledge a bad situation that we are currently in, but need to reassure the emotional self that everything possible is being done and will continue to be done to address it. Then we need to be sure to do so. In these situations, we need to remind the emotional self of things like the low probability of something bad actually happening and that even if the worst happens, we will work together diligently to improve on the worst.

If we are depressed, our conversations should be ones that commiserate and validate feelings by agreeing that "Yes, So-and-So *is* the biggest jerk on the planet." We can also agree that whatever happened was definitely not fair (even if we know that life is not fair). We must clearly inform our emotional self that he/she is not the one at fault. Rather, we can take responsibility for not having processed its feelings in a correct and/or timely manner. We can take responsibility for having been lost in our own victim consciousness and having failed to deliver messages of truth and hope. We can admit to the reality that we are neither omniscient nor omnipotent; we are simply human and prone to mistakes. If nobody is particularly at fault, we can at least establish a sympathetic bond and muddle through together.

When necessary, our conversations should be apologetic for saying and doing some of the terrible things we have. We should make it clear that we are sorry we have subjected our emotional self to so much pain, scared it so many times, and been such a poor caregiver. We must let it know that we are so sorry we have been abusive and that we have expected so much from it when we could not even be bothered to hear its cries. We must apologize for abandoning it and vow to never leave it again.

Even though we do need to sometimes commiserate with the emotional self, we have to also maintain the strength of the parental role. Like any child that needs structure from someone older and wiser, the emotional self needs us to provide it. Consequently, it needs statements of leadership, clarity, strength, and wisdom. We must speak to it from this position.

Sometimes challenges must be made to the emotional self to shake it out of its defeated victim position. We have to remind it that the two of us are not quitters — that giving up is not what we do. It is like we are delivering a reality check to the emotional self. Our emotional self may be wallowing around in the illusion of weakness, victimhood, and failure, but this has nothing to do with what we know it is capable of. We know because we have seen it rise to a challenge many times before. At present, it has simply lost its way, and we need to bring it home immediately.

When we get very depressed or anxious, it is almost like we are in a daze. We live in a constant state of self-loathing and/or apprehension with an ongoing torrent of negative self-talk streaming all the time. We lose any semblance of strength. In fact, we do not even realize that we are so fully lost in this state until serious, focused, positive self-talk starts to happen.

Because of this, when speaking to the emotional self, it is best to concentrate deeply and be extremely resolute in what we are saying. We cannot just make a quick statement and then quit. We need determination and tenacity. We need laser-like communication. This need not be a pressuring event where instantaneous results are expected, but it does need to be one that carries clear intention. Our communication to the emotional self can be nothing more than letting it know that every time it drops back into futility, we will be there to drag it back to hopefulness. This in itself can be quite helpful.

Some people like to talk to the emotional self through the saying or writing of affirmations, which are positive, affirming statements about oneself and one's life. These can be wonderful; however, they must be done in a serious and focused manner. We need to think of our statements to the emotional self as going somewhere and as being received. It is like throwing a baseball and paying close attention to the follow-through. We cannot just talk aimlessly. We need focused intention here.

Sometimes the emotional self will reject new thought processes/affirmations if they seem too fantastic to believe. It gets the impression that we are lying to it. We can repeat our affirmations all day long, and the emotional self will say, "Yeah, right!" In such cases, our affirmations need to be moderated to be in the range of believability. This is fine; we can always work our way up.

The emotional self does not realize that when new patterns of thinking are introduced (as with affirmations), new neurological pathways are formed that reflect the new thought process. We are physically altered to think more positively and thus feel more hopeful even if the old, unused pathways still remain. We need not be stuck with old ways of thinking and feeling because our brains have plasticity and can be molded to new ways of being.

Affirmations are less acceptable to the emotional self when we have not first listened to its feelings and allowed them room to move. It does not allow anything positive when all the negative feeling it is holding is as yet unheard. However, once there has been a sympathetic ear lent to the emotional self, it will make room for new thought. Then it will start to feel better.

Here are a few things that are helpful to tell our emotional self:

- We're going to be okay.
- We're safe and secure.
- Change can be good. Let's give it a chance.
- Let's not take this personally. Others say and do things that are mostly all about themselves.
- Our first loss is our best loss. Let's accept it and move on to the next thing.
- Life is cyclical. There's never a winter that isn't followed by a spring.
- We can tolerate our feelings. People don't die from uncomfortable feelings.
- Let's step back and pause for a moment. Feelings are transitory; they can't stay at a high level of intensity forever.
- Anxiety is just a high level of adrenaline. It's nothing to be scared of.
- Let's try to see things differently.
- We're going to start asking for what we want or need because others can't read our minds.
- Sorry I frightened you with a bunch of scary thoughts.
- We don't have to control everything in order to be okay.

- We have great creative powers.
- I'll help you with any concerns you might have.
- Together we can make excellent decisions for our future. We're a great team.
- Don't worry. I'll give you a say. You'll always be heard.
- Let's see if we can turn your outrage into a constructive plan.
- Don't worry. I won't let you go off half-cocked. I won't let you look bad. I won't let you undermine yourself.
- We have to determine if whatever we are about to do or say is going to help us reach our goal in this matter.
- I know my thoughts are only part of the equation. I need your input as well.

Chapter 15

BEING THE CENTER OF OUR UNIVERSE

Self-attack is not only related to how we are redirecting our anger, how we are or are not acknowledging our primary feelings, and how we are using our thought processes, but it is also related to how we experience ourselves to be positioned in our universe. Do we see ourselves as being the center of our universe or as living on the fringe of it? How does this positioning affect our capacity for self-care? Theodore Isaac Rubin discusses this in his excellent book, *Compassion and Self-Hate*.[1] Some of the highlights in combination with my own thoughts will be summarized here.

Before we start our discussion, it should be noted that there is a difference in seeing ourselves as being the center of *the* universe and seeing ourselves as being the center of *our* universe. The former intimates that we think we rule the entire universe with omnipotence, but the latter suggests that we do not think of ourselves as omnipotent so much as being in charge of our own personal universe. While Dr. Rubin did not make a distinction between the two, it is salient to this discussion.

Let's start our discussion by taking a look at the good aspects of holding a central position in *our* universe. Holding a central position in our universe can be a good thing in that if we experience ourselves to be the center of our universe, we tend to see ourselves as the prevailing power in our lives. We also tend to see ourselves as the parties who are responsible for fulfilling our own needs. We are not overly dependent on others to validate us and bring value to our lives. Our locus of control tends to be more internal than external, which is a good thing.

When we perceive ourselves to be the center of our universe, we do not feel like we are living somewhere on the outskirts of our lives, anxiously waiting for others to inform us of our worth or to give us permission to take care of ourselves. Being the center of our own universe is the opposite of being in a dependent position. It is also the position that allows us to know our own needs and engage in acts of loving self-care.

Being the center of our universe helps promote a strong ego and high self-esteem. From this position we are not desperately searching for a sense of self because we already experience ourselves to have a self. We have formed an identity as an individual separate from the rest of the universe. We already exist and hopefully are in the process of getting to know ourselves better each day.

When we are the center of our universe, we tend to remain comfortable wherever we go because we take the center of our universe with us. It is always present, and there is a cognizance of how to proceed in new circumstances without a loss of self. We remain the central observer of all within our lives, and we remain the responsible party for our own comfort and self-care. Consequently, there is no ensuing panic when circumstances shift. This is because we rely on our self rather than the presence, good will, and feedback of other people.

When we are the center of our universe, we retain the right...

- to say *no*.
- to change our minds.
- to choose for ourselves.
- to fail.
- to not know everything.

- to enjoy pleasurable activities.
- to do things on our own timetable.
- to exclude individuals who are not good for us.
- to not pressure ourselves.
- to not forgive others until we feel ready.
- to live our lives authentically rather than live our lives performing for others.
- to let others take responsibility for themselves.

All of these good aspects of being the center of our own universe are made possible by achieving the level of development in which we have separated and individuated from our primary caregiver. In this process we have come to know our self as a sovereign entity separate from the whole. If we were still merged with our primary caregiver, we would not even be aware of having a universe of our own, much less the benefits of being the center of our own universe. This is because when we are very young, we exist in an enmeshed, unindividuated state with our primary caregiver. We have no way to know that we are individuals, much less individuals worthy of our own self-care. Nor do we know that anyone else exists or that they, too, must be cared for and respected. Instead, we exist in a merged state of primary narcissism as the unchallenged, omnipotent center of *the* universe — an innocent state, but a narcissistic one nonetheless. In this state of oneness, *our* universe is *the* universe; there is no distinction between the two.

In this state we are focused exclusively on getting our own needs met, which unfortunately happens at the expense of others. We do not even know others are there, much less have an awareness of their efforts, struggles, frailties, fatigue, etc. However, with normal, healthy development, this merged, self-absorbed state gives way to an awareness of both self and others. Happily, in finding ourselves, we have found others as well. In our new state of selfhood, we learn not take others for granted, using them only for our own purposes. We learn how to relate in a give-and-take fashion.

Some of us, however, do not make it through the separation/ individuation stage successfully. We psychologically remain fixated there no matter how old we get. Then we spend the rest of our lives depending on others whom we see as extensions of ourselves and waiting for others to feed us, fulfill us, and define us. We also spend it largely thinking only of ourselves. Even though we do not mean to, we function primarily as narcissists. Here we are face to face with the negative aspect of seeing ourselves as *the* center of the universe.

It is vital that we successfully reach an individuated level of development so that we can shed our innocent yet narcissistic personas. We need to figure out how to get lives of our own and how to take care of ourselves without taking advantage of others.

Sometimes there is confusion over whether or not self-care constitutes a self-absorbed position or simply a self-respecting one. This can stop us from taking care of ourselves. Certainly we should take a good look at ourselves and make sure we are not coming from the former. It is never a pretty sight to witness the actions of highly selfish people who fancy themselves to be on the right track. However, if we know that we truly have the ability to see the position of others, the struggles of others, and the rights of others, then we should rest easy with our efforts to help ourselves. We are most likely well within the bounds of compassion for all.

To help clear up any uncertainty, here are a few comparisons between enmeshed narcissists and individuals.

- Narcissists who are trying to get their needs met rely on others to deliver their narcissistic supplies. Individuals rely on themselves.
- Narcissists unwittingly use up others. Healthy, self-caring individuals use up no one.

- Narcissists care little for others. Healthy, self-caring individuals care both for others and for self.
- Narcissists think it is a pleasure for others to do things for them. Individuals think no such thing.
- Narcissists have disturbed interpersonal relationships. Individuals who care for self while still being aware of their impact on others have fulfilling relationships.
- Narcissists cannot deal with the word *no*. Individuals can.
- Narcissists think that what belongs to others is also theirs; there are no lines of distinction. Individuals are aware of boundaries and see what belongs to others.
- Narcissists get wounded when others do not deliver or set a boundary. Individuals do not.

Aside from narcissistic self-absorption, a major hazard in experiencing ourselves to be *the* center of the universe is that as the center of the universe, we think that we are connected to all happenings in that universe. It is like there is an invisible string emanating from every happening in the universe that is attached to us. We end up with billions of imaginary strings attached to us. Consequently, it seems to us that every happening in the universe has something to do with us; every one of them is a result of something we did or did not do. This applies to both good and bad occurrences.

The problem with this is that since we fail to realize that separate others are present, we cannot see that some of our causative strings should be attached to someone else. Therefore, we fail to register the fact that some life events have nothing to do with us and that the world is going to be whatever it is independent of us. What we must accept is that we never had nor will have the degree of control over life's happenings that we would like to have. We only have control over our own actions and our own responses, i.e., we only have control over our own universe.

This is a very important concept to grasp because if we insist on viewing every happening as being tied to our own actions, worth, thoughts, or feelings, we will end up taking responsibility for all kinds of things that have nothing to do with us. We will end up feeling like every bad thing that happens to us is our fault. We will endlessly tell ourselves that we could have done this or that, and if we only had, such an event would not have occurred. After all, if only we exist, who else can be blamed for whatever goes wrong? It has to be our fault.

If we adopt this world view, we will end up feeling guilty over many things. We will also end up with a reduced sense of worth, for supposedly we failed to do something that could have been done. We also failed to be someone we should have been. We are certain that we could have been more capable, more loveable, and/or more aware of something that was happening. We could have been smarter, stronger, healthier, richer, and more powerful. We could have been perfect.

Thus far, we have discussed narcissists who think they head up *the* universe as a by-product of lack of individuation. This is called primary narcissism. Such individuals are not bad, but are simply developmentally impaired. We might even see them as clueless (think babies). However, there is another kind of narcissism, known as secondary narcissism, which produces a different type of narcissist. Secondary narcissists are not necessarily unindividuated, but are preoccupied with covering up their own weaknesses. To be more accurate, secondary narcissists are engrossed with covering up their own self-loathing. In fact, they are pretty much poster children for self-hate.

Narcissists who are suffering from secondary narcissism usually have a difficult time being imperfect human beings, which is a very self-hating position. They are fixated on achieving an ideal self in an effort to cover up their weaknesses and fears. Their grandiose actions and consistent strivings for power are just attempts to build a huge superstructure of fabulousness around themselves to cover up their fragility and self-loathing. In fact, this kind of narcissism has been called a cloak for self-hate.[2]

Secondary narcissists technically realize that there are separate others, but they treat people like objects to be used rather than as individuals with feelings. They do this partially because they are so busy trying to compensate for their flaws that there is no real registration of others. Moreover, secondary narcissists cannot achieve any degree of self-care. That would involve ministering to the actual, flawed self. Instead, the needs of the actual self are pretty much eclipsed by focusing on the idealized self, which is not even a real self. Rather, it is an aggrandized image of self that they project out to the world.

Both primary and secondary narcissists take up a lot of space in the universe (one thinks that he or she *is* the universe and the other tries to be larger than life within the universe). Thus, both are at risk for self-attack for different reasons. While primary narcissists are at risk for self-attack because they think all happenings are tied to them, secondary narcissists are at risk for self-attack because they must stay larger than life and cannot accept that they are imperfectly human.

While the antidote to self-hate/self-attack with primary narcissism is individuation, the antidote to self-hate with secondary narcissism is to embrace and accept the human condition rather than attempt to escape it. It is to. . .

- become fully human.
- allow our real self to be seen.
- allow the deep relief of imperfection.
- indulge in deep, self-caring behaviors.
- work with our anxiety about a crazy world without having to control every inch of it.
- make the shift from being the center of *the* universe to being the center of *our own* universe.

Chapter 16

THE ACTUAL SELF, THE IDEALIZED SELF, AND THE REVILED SELF

In this chapter we will explore the characteristics of the actual self, the idealized self, and the reviled self. We will also take a look at how the discrepancies between them serve as a portal for self-attack as set forth by Dr. Theodore Isaac Rubin. [1]

The actual self is our authentic self, complete with both strengths and weaknesses. The idealized self is our embellished self. It is who we either think we are or hope to be in the future. The reviled self is the hated version of self. Any time there is a discrepancy among these three versions of self, there is an opportunity for self-attack.

The idealized self usually involves outrageously high expectations, unrealistic goals, dreams of glorious success, visions of perfection, illusions about our capabilities, and inner mandates about how things should be done. It presupposes that we are above the human condition and incapable of a bad decision. The idealized self is fraught with arrogance and has been termed by Karen Horney as a "pride system." [2] The idealized self holds much potential for self-hate because no human being can live up to it and because other people cannot consistently give us what we need to keep our inflated illusion of self going.

Despite its over-inflated nature, the idealized self is not always experienced as arrogant or prideful. It can simply feel like a pressure to succeed, to live up to our potential, or to fulfill others' expectations of us. It can also be experienced as an effort to be godly, a compulsive striving for perfection, or an obligation to put ourselves last. We sometimes even experience our "pride system" to be a good thing.

However we experience it, the scope and intensity of the idealized self is too broad and too intense for inner peace to exist. It is such a departure from reality that true joy in any achievement is impossible. It counters the actual self, which allows true happiness in the achievement of our goals and makes it entirely possible to strive for our best without being compulsive.

If we are to keep self-attack at bay, we must strive to stay as closely aligned as possible with the actual self. It does not matter at all what the actual self contains. It only matters that we claim the actual self as our own true self and that we always strive to give it care and comfort. Any movement away from it is a movement toward self-hate.

The gap between the actual self and the idealized self tends to create great anxiety — the wider the gap, the greater the anxiety. This is because the escalating fear of exposure becomes overwhelming. There is just too much to protect and too much at stake to ever relax. As a result, we sentence ourselves to an ongoing state of trepidation and vulnerability.

It is also possible to have a discrepancy between the actual self and the reviled self. The reviled self is a hated version of the self that is experienced as an unworthy failure. It is always the weak one, the one at fault, the one that is never good enough, the one that does not deserve much. It represents all of the parts of self that we dislike, that we judge, and that we deny the opportunity to move.

The gap between the actual self and the reviled self presents a more direct form of self-hate than the gap between the actual self and the idealized self. With the former, the actual self is constantly under siege — not to perform brilliantly, but to take anything good for itself in the face of unyielding self-denigration. We have an ongoing struggle to trust ourselves and to see ourselves as having value. Nothing that is done is ever good enough and no credit is ever received.

The reviled self represents not only our neuroses, but also our tendencies toward masochism. It can be used to reduce expectations, prevent criticism, avoid choosing a better path for us, undo unacceptable thoughts and feelings, and provide penance for supposed inner and outer infractions. It denies the actual self an opportunity to use its strength to speak up, step out, and make a good life for itself.

The gap between the actual self and the reviled self also creates an exposure factor. We do not fear that we will be found to be lesser than the image we protect, but that we will be unveiled as the loathsome, fully unacceptable person we think we are. This alone would make it worth our while to unearth our supposedly unacceptable parts and meet them with compassion. Nothing need be reviled if it is met with gentle observation, empathy, and understanding.

Despite the fact that the actual self/reviled self version of disparate selves presents a different kind of dilemma than does the actual self/idealized self version, it is still a deviation from the reality of the actual self. It is still falseness rather than realness. Even though at opposite polarities, both versions of actual versus something- other-than-actual are forms of self-hate birthed and kept alive by an inner self-attacker who simply cannot abide authenticity.

In reality, all of these selves are but aspects of our psyche. Yet it can be very helpful to work with them separately so that we can get a better idea of how we invite self-attack. The bottom line is that whether we are overinflating ourselves to protect our vulnerabilities or denigrating ourselves to reduce expectations, deflect criticism, and punish the self for having weaknesses, both positions are departures from loving acceptance of the actual self.

Chapter 17

ILLUSIONS AND SELF-ATTACK

An illusion is a fantasy about self, someone else, or the world at large. It is a form of deception that gives us a misleading idea about reality. Illusions are usually compensatory in that they make up for qualities, abilities, and life circumstances that we do not actually have. They are used to make life more acceptable, more tolerable, and less frightening. Aside from the innocent fantasies of childhood, illusions can be quite destructive and tend to debilitate the actual self. They delay our emotional maturation as well as our ability to cope with life by keeping our focus away from reality. They also fuel self-attack because we cannot possibly live up to their over-inflated version of reality.

Illusions about our self usually involve some version of omniscience or omnipotence.[1] Omniscience has to do with complete knowledge, awareness, insight, and wisdom; omnipotence has to do with unlimited power, authority, influence, and control. Together they conjure up visions of an infallible, invincible, potent, all-knowing, perfected individual. To this we aspire.

Illusions about the self oftentimes involve great virtuosity. We entertain the fantasy that we are saintly, all-giving, all-sacrificing, benevolent, all-forgiving, understanding, and pure. We are nice guys and gals, free of malice, anger, falseness, or envy. We are above the fray, above the masses, above the vicissitudes of life.

In such cases we are busy escaping our actual self, all the while ensuring continued self-attack as the disparity between reality and illusion makes itself apparent.

We can also have illusions about ourselves in the opposite direction, convincing ourselves that we are weak, incompetent, unknowledgeable, and powerless when we are not. These illusions, though not overinflated versions of reality, still invite self-attack in that they lead us to believe in limitations that do not exist.

Illusions about others typically involve idealization. We see them as all-knowing, all-powerful, brilliant, special, caring individuals who can protect our interests and keep us safe from harm. This is not only the case with parents, but also with doctors, lawyers, therapists, teachers, leaders, and lovers. We need to feel like there is someone there who is superhuman and will never let us down. Strangely, children can also fall into this category as we idealize them beyond all reason. These children are idealized not to keep us safe from harm, but to fulfill our own fantasies; they are simply the recipient of our own idealized projections about ourselves. [2]

Illusions about the world at large include the fantasy that the past can be made up for, i.e., there is a place and time for perfect justice in this world. We fancy that our wounds from past injustices will be healed by others getting their just desserts. In the meantime, there is too much focus on injustice-collecting, proof of suffering, and waiting for that mythical day of payback. This destroys happiness in the here and now, which can never be good enough to undo the past. [3]

Another illusion about the world at large is that it is possible to repeatedly achieve peak sexual experience with each intimate encounter. However, in the real world there is no possibility of perfect sex (much less repetitively occurring perfect sex); this is a destructive myth that has been propagated by our society. It ruins the joy of actual sex due to the gap between reality and fantasy. It causes self-consciousness and performance anxiety by taking us out of our present moment. Some sexual fantasies (as promulgated by pornography) go so far beyond the realm of reality that compared to them everything else will most likely be disappointing. [4]

Also, it is possible to confuse sexual need with our other needs, thus exaggerating its role in our lives. It is not uncommon to substitute sexual fantasy for whatever else is felt to be a deprivation. This can lead to the illusion that sexual satisfaction will fix everything in our lives when it will not. [5]

In a related vein is the illusion that it is possible to have a perfect connection with another human being (physically, mentally, emotionally, and spiritually). In a sense, we are seeking merger with him or her. We think that such a union will bring us feelings of deep contentment and security. The last time that was a possibility was in the womb! Yet we spend inordinate amounts of time trying to recreate it within our relationships. We need to remain cognizant of the fact that in this lifetime we are supposed to be individuating (becoming separate, conscious individuals), not trying to recreate an illusory womb where we can remain safely merged with someone else.

This does not mean that we will not achieve many lovely interludes of emotional connection within our lifetimes. Certainly we will. What it does mean is that we need to be content with the imperfect nature of these connections and not be too reliant on them for our sense of safety and well-being.

Another illusion we like to entertain about the world at large is that there exists a state of nirvana-like happiness that involves sustained, climactic highs. In reality happiness tends to be intermittent, relative to many uncontrollable factors, and more comfortably content than exhilarating. [6] There is no chance for perfected, ongoing happiness; there are only times of comfort and relaxation that leave a sense of well-being. We should not be seeking addictive happiness highs. Such an unrealistic pursuit is too pressuring and intimidating for any human being to endure.

There are a few other illusions along the sustained happiness theme. Many of us hold the illusion that money brings never-ending happiness and perpetual problem-free living. Some think it may even provide immortality. In a related vein is an illusion about popularity curing all ills, one about success as an entryway to a rarefied realm of the satisfied elite, one about consistently winning in competitions as a method of achieving self-worth, and one about the good life filled with beautiful people as a pathway to being powerful, chosen, and "special." All of these destroy reality, lead us to obsessional ways of functioning, and keep us from accepting our actual selves.

As you can see, illusions, beliefs, and expectations are linked. Once we buy into an illusion, we generate all kinds of beliefs about what we should or should not be doing. However, since illusions are terrible misperceptions of reality, they lead us to believe all the wrong things, which then give rise to skewed expectations. They lead us to believe that we can and must function above the realm of human possibility. This belief in superhuman functioning serves as an overarching theme which leads to a host of more specific beliefs that work in its service.

Some of the more specific superhuman beliefs might sound like:

- I believe I must be consistently brilliant.
- I believe I should always be forgiving.
- I believe I should always be positive, upbeat, and nonjudgmental.
- I believe I should be able to solve all my problems by myself.
- I believe I should always be focused, competent, and capable.
- I believe I can achieve anything.
- I believe I can always be a winner.

We concoct all sorts of demanding, self-hating beliefs about ourselves accompanied by ridiculously exorbitant expectations, but if we are willing to take a look at which illusions we hold that cause us to apply such stringent beliefs and expectations to ourselves, we can successfully circumvent some very painful, self-critical feelings.

A powerful way to move away from illusion and toward self-acceptance is to live within the realm of human possibility.[7] This means giving up our preoccupation with an idealized self and instead starting to live as normal human beings who are subject to the limitations of this world. In this process we will need to lower our lofty standards, limit our overzealous goals, and reduce our grandiose expectations.[8] This is not to suggest that we allow our standards to become substandard, our goals to be uninspired, or our expectations to be lowered to our detriment. It simply means that we need to move into a realm that is full of attainable possibilities rather than a realm of guaranteed failure. This will allow us a sense of hope, fulfillment, strength, and peace.

In our efforts to keep our goals within the achievable range, it is important to pay attention not only to the nature of our beliefs and expectations, but also to their course. Sometimes we start off with a mostly realistic, well-intentioned belief/expectation that, taken too far, loses its validity. Perhaps we have started off with a relatively high but reasonable standard for success and allowed it to morph into a grandiose scheme for unlimited success. Or perhaps we have started off legitimately supporting a loved one and allowed this to transform into a masochistic sacrifice of self. Our course has now been altered due to too much of a good thing. A valid belief and standard for success has turned into an invalid one. Flexibility, intuition, self-care, and presence of mind are paramount when we are attempting to advance our goals without ending up in a self-hating world of illusion.

Having to live up to unrealistic standards, goals, and expectations is a vicious and ruthless endeavor. It is also a vicious and ruthless thing to impose on others. Such a pursuit is cruel not only in its initial demands for superior performance, but also in the need it imposes to consistently reproduce impossible levels of achievement or unfailingly be a superhuman being. It is merciless in that it sends us on a never-ending wild-goose chase, constantly pushing us toward the next superlative "high."

The craving for a continual high indicates the presence of addiction. Unrealistic standards, goals, and expectations feed addiction; they amount to a coercion of the self to keep performing at unrealistic levels in pursuit of the next high. [9] Rather than obsessively chase peak experiences, we need to work compassionately with our own authentic self and guard against the need for image-driven highs. We need to watch out not only for the high itself but for the pressure to continually reproduce it as well, whether it is our quest for the high of continued success, continued popularity, continued status, or continued anything.

One thing we can do to stay away from unexcelled functioning and addictive highs is to allow ourselves to be ordinary and to enjoy our ordinariness. The word *ordinary* in this sense does not mean dreary, dull, or trite; it means normal, commonplace, and average. We do not have to be doing something amazing all the time. Nor do we have to be scintillating, deep, intellectually challenging, funny, witty, or pithy in our observations all the time. It is all too demanding and pressuring. We might also allow ourselves to enjoy the simple things in life like a beautiful sunset, a chat with a friend, or a walk in the park. There is something wonderful about being able to relax and participate in an activity that is unremarkable but satisfying. If we ever hear ourselves criticizing this kind of enjoyment, we may be in self-hating territory.

In our quest to reduce impossible standards and strivings, it is good to live our lives in what Theodore Isaac Rubin calls "compassionate shades of gray." This means that we stay away from black-and-white functioning and instead see ourselves as complex beings whose emotional lives are exemplified by inconsistency, incongruity, and varying shades of all kinds of feelings. [10] Likewise, we must come to see ourselves as beings whose mental lives are characterized by all kinds of cognitive errors that cause confusion, conflict, and misperceptions. The self is far from simplistic and should not be approached in a polarized, black-and-white manner. A black-and-white vision of self is just another false illusion presenting us with a stack of ridiculous *shoulds* leading to absurdly unrealistic goals and expectations.

Compassionate shades of gray ask that we not speak about ourselves and others in superlative terms. Everything does not have to be great, fabulous, fantastic, super, wonderful, marvelous, brilliant, or incredible. These superlatives usually indicate the agenda of a self-hating perfectionist, which must be turned aside. We need to be careful not to demand greatness of ourselves and others. We must learn to make do with a human-proportioned self and a normal life with expected ups and downs. When our true moments of greatness emerge from time to time, they can be savored, but they should never be our main focus in life.

Becoming familiar with the pride positions of our idealized self can also be very helpful in recognizing our overinflated illusions. Each time we discover a pride position within ourselves we unearth an illusion that we hold. This may be a pride position of saintliness, greatness, smartness, successfulness, specialness, kindness, intuitiveness, self-awareness, wisdom, functioning ability, etc. Each time we make an effort to give up this pride position, we are able to somewhat relinquish the illusion. Eventually, we are able to discover reality and replace our self-hating demands with compassion. [11]

Noticing the presence of anxiety within ourselves can help us discover and relinquish our illusions as well. Anxiety can be present for a variety of reasons, but one of the main reasons is that we have bumped into an illusion that needs to be surrendered. This can be an illusion about our self, about another, or about the world at large. If it is about our self, it means that the gap between our illusory, idealized self and our real, actual self has become too disparate and conflictual for comfort. If it is about someone else, the gap between our idealized version of that person and reality has become too disappointing, frightening, or worrisome to easily tolerate. The same holds true for the gap between reality and our illusions about the world at large; once seen, the gap between the two can leave us feeling so frightened, disenchanted, and impotent that we may feel like we are having a nervous breakdown.

However, once we have identified the illusion, realistic disillusionment and compassionate relinquishment of the illusion can follow. [12] This process is made easier by working through our primary feelings of fear, anger, sadness, and helplessness rather than twisting them into self-hating recriminations, guilt, shame, and depression. No one should be expected to relinquish an illusion without attending to the feelings that accompany the loss of it. In the long run, grieving is empowering.

Another thing we can do to keep ourselves in the realm of realism is to examine the maturity level of our expectations. If we are not to be consistently disappointed and self-attacking, our expectations must be somewhat mature. They cannot reflect our need for constant narcissistic support nor can they reflect all of our childhood dreams and longings. If they do, we will be consistently and bitterly disappointed.

We also need to look at the intensity level of our expectations. If we are not to be in a constant state of despair, disappointment, and self-loathing, our expectations need to be more like preferences rather than unyielding demands for specific outcomes. Of course there are some expectations that we cannot compromise on, such as the expectation that we be treated with consideration and respect. However, many of our expectations should have a little wiggle room. Our entire sense of self-esteem and well-being should not depend on whether or not someone lived up to our unyielding demands or whether we lived up to our own. The act of changing demands to preferences is a potent tool in our efforts to accept reality and to be at peace.

When working with illusions, we can err in either the direction of having expectations that are too high or too low. Expectations that are too high usually emerge from overinflated illusions held by the ideal self while those that are too low usually emerge from the self-hating illusions of the reviled self. Expectations that are too high put a huge burden on us and those around us; they place us in the fragile position of needing them to be filled in order for us to be okay. Expectations that are too low either result in a failure to live up to our potential or situations in which others are allowed to harm us and run all over us with impunity. Both invite victimization and reinforce our unworthiness.

If we can keep our expectations modulated, somewhat mature, suited to the constraints of the present moment, and in the preference zone rather than the demand zone, we will find our level of self-attack greatly diminished. Otherwise, we will have singlehandedly managed to set both ourselves and others up to fail and destined ourselves to feel repeatedly undervalued and unfulfilled.

Sometimes when there is a new awareness about the nature of reality, it remains difficult to relinquish our former illusion. This is the case because acceptance of the new reality must follow its acknowledgment, and sometimes we are unable to accept the truth. Perhaps it is too terrorizing, too grievous, or too difficult to acknowledge that we have spent most of our lives chasing a lie. It can also be difficult to accept a new reality because sometimes recriminations and harsh judgments of our self can follow the realization that we are neither omniscient nor omnipotent. This is largely due, however, to insufficient processing of the primary feelings, particularly fear and helplessness. Whatever the case, we need to be patient with ourselves and give ourselves a little time to adjust to our new reality.

Self-attack over our inability to live up to our illusions can be very stubborn and resistant, but we do at least need to attempt to make a change in the way we think about life and the things we demand of ourselves. The list of *shoulds* that we hold up for ourselves as a standard is both daunting and unrealistic. We need to give ourselves a break and dare to be human. We also need to give this latitude to others.

Chapter 18

NOT KNOWING AS A FORM OF SELF-ATTACK

The illusion of omniscience presupposes that we are both aware of everything and that we know everything. Rationally, this concept is so absurd that we can easily pronounce it invalid, yet we are willing to accept less obvious versions of it that result in unreasonable (if not impossible) goals, standards, and expectations. These subtle versions of sagacity might not sound as grandiose as the word *omniscience*, yet they are adaptations of it and must be acknowledged as such. This is the case because eventually our inability to attain and/or maintain such overinflated standards (no matter how subtly they are posed) will lead to self-attack.

Such adaptations of omniscience usually involve something we think we should have known either about ourselves, someone else, or a life situation. It can also involve a decision or behavior that we have engaged in. When we hear ourselves uttering the phrase "I should have known," this is an indicator that we are in close proximity to a belief in our own omniscience. We are either telling ourselves that it was possible to foresee things in a prescient manner (and we just failed to do so) or that we should have had total recall of all that we do know. It also presumes that there were no other impinging factors in play.

In order to get past this idea that we "should have known," we have to first acknowledge that we have strayed into omniscience territory. We may not think we have, but we have. The second thing we have to do is question our assumption, however subtle, that omniscience is ever a valid possibility. The third thing we have to do is to consider all the other factors that are in play when we are unable to perform to the level that we aspire. Fourth, we have to forgive ourselves for not knowing everything, i.e., we must consent to being human.

Let's take a look at the assumption that it is possible to be aware of everything. The truth is that human beings are extremely limited in their scope of awareness. Our defense system blocks huge amounts of incoming information, and our faulty thought processes (beliefs, transferences, misperceptions, etc.) skew what does come through. In addition, we are mostly reliant on our five senses, which limits our ability to gain awareness through other extrasensory pathways. Most of us are not even aware that there are other pathways for awareness/knowledge, and those who are aware of them certainly have not yet developed all the possibilities for using them. In fact, humans are more unaware of things than they are aware of them. It is a given; we all lack awareness in one way or another. We all have areas of not knowing.

Not knowing something can and usually does result in behaviors that we engage in from a place of blindness and now wish we had not done. Typically they leave us mortified beyond belief and scrambling to redeem ourselves. These behaviors brought on by not knowing are often seen in one's youth, but can follow us into adulthood if we fail to gain self-awareness. Oftentimes they result in tremendous self-judgment and self-loathing that can leave us very depressed.

Since these types of unconscious behaviors are not willful, we cannot categorize them as purposeful behaviors. They come from a place of obliviousness and are driven by biological needs, emotional needs, anxiety, depression, pain, immaturity, low self-esteem, and/or inexperience. Here we are unconsciously trying to achieve a sense of physical and emotional equilibrium more than deliberately hurt anyone with our behaviors. While it is true that our impulsive strivings to reinstate our inner equilibrium can result in behaviors we would never condone in our current state of awareness, at the time we are engaging in these behaviors, we are innocent.

Still, we excoriate ourselves for not having known. We deride ourselves for not having been perfect. We attack ourselves rather than face the painful consequences of our behaviors or the specter that someone may find out and judge or abandon us. We attack ourselves because once we have gained awareness, we cannot bear to know that we have hurt someone as badly as we have. We attack ourselves because we are good people who did not act in alignment with our inner core of goodness, and this hurts us greatly.

Oprah Winfrey has shared a gem that Maya Angelou once told her, and that is, "When you know better, you do better." [1] This is so true, for we can only act in accordance with what we know. We should let this truth in.

Not knowing better is not a criminal offense. If we ever really knew the degree of our pain, need, and anxiety that underlies our blind behaviors, we would drop to our knees in deep sorrow for ourselves. We would wail over the wrongful and vicious beatings we have visited upon ourselves, appalled at the sadistic way we have thrashed ourselves over every little imperfection. We would look at ourselves with deep remorse and undying compassion. We would take pity upon ourselves. We would have mercy and understanding.

Yet mercy and understanding are not easy to achieve; it is hard to register just how many disappointments and hurts we have had throughout our lives without blaming ourselves. It is difficult to acknowledge how unloved we have felt, how misunderstood we have been, or how unsupported we have been without experiencing an element of self-hatred. It is harder still to face how broken and needy we may be as a result of all this. It is this broken, needy self that we judge so harshly and that is deeply in need of our love and understanding.

Once we can face the broken self without recrimination, we can get on with life in a much happier way. We can do it in a manner that does not demand fulfillment of unrealistic goals, impossible expectations, and perfected self-awareness. We can do it being the protector of our self rather than its executioner.

Sometimes we ask ourselves why life would bring us experiences that exceed our ability to effectively cope. Given our level of development, such experiences cannot be faced with maturity and knowingness. After all, this pretty much guarantees that we will behave in a manner that we later wish we had not. Upon giving it thought, it seems that learning through our own experience is the only real way that we absorb anything. The situations that we do so poorly with are presented for our growth. They are learning laboratories, not tests. We were never expected to do well within them. If we have muddled through with a new awareness or a new learning, we have done well.

In these learning situations, it is good to be humble. In the overall scheme of things, we are still children figuring out the basics. We are not perfected beings here to prove how unflawed we are. We probably would not even be here on this planet if we were perfected beings.

What gets in the way of our humility? Perhaps it is the way we take in strict religious, parental, or educational training, always striving to be so good and pure. Yet truly perfected beings do not strive simply for good qualities. They are perfected because they have learned that perfection is having all aspects of self and loving each and every one of them. Perfection is not defined by goodness. It is defined by wholeness.

Ironically, when we are attacking ourselves for one imperfect aspect of our self or another, we are way off the path of perfection. Instead, we need to head straight for our imperfections, embrace them, and smile upon them with great tenderness. Then we will be back on the track to both perfection through wholeness and forgiveness for not knowing.

In our quest for wholeness and self-forgiveness, we might consider the possibility that all of life's situations (no matter how badly we do with them) are part of our established path. We could not be here doing what we are doing if it were not established. It is all part of our intended growth path no matter how badly we think we are messing things up. This alone can be very comforting as we come to realize the level of support this universe provides.

Aside from our religious, parental, and educational training, our own narcissism can make it difficult to give up our obsession with goodness and purity. It is tough to admit that we have little, weak, needy, selfish, out-of-control aspects of ourselves. It can be humiliating and embarrassing, especially if these aspects have been criticized by others in our past. However, we need to remember that our narcissistic strivings are mostly about maintaining an image of glorious, transcendent, non-human perfection, power, and control so that we can feel better about ourselves (not because we are megalomaniacs). It would be better to give up protecting our image and get on with the business of getting to know and accept all those supposedly unacceptable things about ourselves.

Sometimes we look back at all that has occurred in our lives and understandably grieve the lost time, the lost relationships, and all the lost opportunities. Truly there can be a lot of loss that we accrue while we are slowly but surely gaining our awareness. Yet all we can do is keep on moving forward, staying present, and doing the best we can. If we do this, the quality of our lives will improve. More than that, if we can just hold steady, remain grateful for what we do have, and maintain a broad perspective, oftentimes our losses are restored in the most amazing ways.

So let's not get too carried away with the glories of instant awareness, insisting that our inner child know things it cannot yet possibly know. Let's be content to be growth-oriented human beings who valiantly seek and patiently participate in our own individualized plan. We must try to be persistent seekers and humble learners.

The deep embarrassment, shame, and self-recrimination that can come from not knowing are all forms of self-attack. Consequently, we must work with them as we would any other self-attacking feeling. To find relief, we have to first become aware that we are attacking ourselves, which can be determined by noticing if we are entertaining thoughts or experiencing feelings that are disparaging to our self. Then we must determine what lies beneath these disparaging thoughts and feelings (perhaps shock, disbelief, betrayal, disappointment, disillusionment, loneliness, neediness, anger/rage, sorrow/grief, fear/terror, or helplessness/powerlessness. We must then agree to stop using our self-attack as a shield against these underlying feelings and consent to experiencing them. They may be intense and possibly painful, but not one of them will feel as bad as the original self-recrimination. None of them will involve our worth or lovability. All of them will feel blessed by our willingness to hear them, and all will be helped by the use of our cognitive tools.

When working with our self-attack, it is important to remember that regret and self-recrimination are not synonymous. Regret manifests as a sorrowful feeling of remorse while self-recrimination involves a charge made against an accused. The latter is usually accompanied by self-loathing, guilt, and shame. This is what we are trying to avoid.

Some of us believe that in order to be truly regretful, we must pay penance through self-denial, self-loathing, guilt, shame, and anxiety (even if our behaviors were due to a lack of awareness). Consequently, we think of our self-recrimination as a good thing — that it is somehow balancing our transgressions. Unfortunately, it does nothing of the kind. It just contributes to more self-loathing.

Sometimes we feel the need to pay penance because we are aware of the human need that underlies our regrettable be

We do not understand that we may have acted inappropriately, hurtfully, or stupidly because we were deeply yearning for something. Our behaviors may have been motivated by a need to alleviate our deep loneliness, to be heard and understood, or to feel a human connection. We may have been desperate for validation, searching for worth, or aching for the feeling of being special to somebody. We may have even had the need to release some of our repressed anger or save ourselves from something we deeply feared. None of these things demand self-flagellation, especially if we did not know the needs that motivated our behaviors to begin with.

So often we attack ourselves by saying, "I knew better and did it anyway." However, this is most likely not the case. Granted, we may have intellectually known about the ethics of the situation, but probably did not know about all the underlying emotional factors that led us to our regretted actions. All must be taken into consideration when we start talking about knowing; there are precious few of us who have a conscious, working knowledge of our emotional self. We need to ease up on ourselves for we know a whole lot less about what motivates us than we think we do.

Aside from the way we attack ourselves for our own unconscious behaviors is the way we attack ourselves when someone else behaves unconsciously and hurts us with the things they say and do. This is so common that it might even be considered a universal state of affairs.

Those who hurt us with their lack of awareness do not know what they are doing any more than we know what we are doing when we are bumbling around in the dark. Many of them have no idea how to love. Sadly, they are tremendously lonely people. Yet we relate to them as if they do know how to love, but are just withholding it from us. We then choose to believe that there is something wrong with us; otherwise we would be getting their love. But the reality is that they do not have a clue. We could be perfect and they still would not have a clue.

Much of the time the way they relate to us is from a place of belief about the way this or that should be done (discipline, control, roles played, etc.). Perhaps they relate to us in the way others related to them, which may have been sorely lacking or downright abusive. Then they keep doing it over and over until it dawns on them that they are lonely and this is not working. Sometimes they go a whole lifetime without this realization. Even the most perfect child born to the unaware person can do nothing but provide life experience for that parent from which he or she might eventually learn. We must never measure our own worth against the unaware person whether it is a parent or a friend or a lover. It is such a colossal loss of our time and energy.

Sometimes we strike out to teach these people how to love. We show them what it is. We show them what it looks like. We try to bring them along. Sometimes this works and sometimes it does not. It all depends on their readiness and ability to grow. It also depends on their own life path and the experiences they need to live out. It has no bearing on whether or not we were successful in bringing them along. If they are not ready to know how to love, they are not ready to know how to love ... period.

It can be hard to realize that some individuals whom we have looked up to all our lives as parents, spouses, or friends have been oblivious all along, empty all along, lacking all along. It can be such a shock to realize that we have imbued them with qualities they never had, capabilities they never had, and awareness they never had. It is never easy to see that we have relied on a fantasy and measured our worth against an illusion.

While it is sad and upsetting to realize this, so much of our self-attack fades away with this knowledge and is replaced by not only a sense of compassion for ourselves, but for the offending party as well. If it is someone close to us that we have previously had issues with, our frustrations melt away in the light of our new-found realization. Our hearts go out to their lonely plight. We feel for them even as we know we must set boundaries with them for our own protection. We are saddened over their having gone through a lifetime of emptiness and isolation. Concurrently we are lifted by the knowledge that we were never lacking to begin with and that our worth is intact.

Whether it is we who have erred from a place of obliviousness and/or inexperience or someone else who has erred for the same reasons, it is always best to go forward with the understanding that when we do not know something, we are truly blameless. We may have to contend with the fallout from our actions, and we may have to take responsibility for any damage incurred, but we should not excoriate ourselves for what we did not know. We can only learn from our experience; that will have to be good enough.

Chapter 19

FORGIVENESS AND SELF-ATTACK

In this chapter we will take a look at the role self-attack plays in thwarting forgiveness (whether it be forgiveness of others or forgiveness of the self). While forgiveness of others is important, this will not be the main focus; the main focus will be on forgiveness of others as a byproduct of forgiving the self.

There is a direct relationship between our own self-attack and our inability to forgive others; the more we attack ourselves, the less able we are to forgive others. Usually when attempting to forgive others for their transgressions, our focus is on overcoming our judgments of *them*, thus letting them off the hook. However, the way to actually accomplish forgiveness of others is to let *ourselves* off the hook.

When we are holding judgments against others and cannot seem to forgive them, it can be difficult to see that there is an element of self-attack in play. At first it is not obvious because we are fixated on the offending parties, impugning their actions, actively disliking them, wanting to retaliate, and in general being stuck on our inability to pardon them. But underneath, something else is happening.

Underneath all this focus on the other person, we have most likely been pronouncing ourselves to be unlovable, disposable, forgettable, worthless, unwanted, foolish, meaningless, bad, useless, incompetent, contemptible, shameful, guilty, disgusting, or deficient. We may be feeling like a big nothing, a big failure, or a big disappointment. Most likely we are straining under the yoke of being used, abused, oppressed, invaded, kicked aside, misunderstood, vilified, scapegoated, and/or humiliated, and are now redirecting our outrage for the perpetrators to ourselves.

Once this happens, we need to get busy working to turn our anger around. We have already discussed elsewhere how to identify and assign our anger to the correct person(s) before it gets redirected and morphed into bullets with our names on them. We also know how to identify the feelings of fear, sorrow, and helplessness that lie beneath our anger. However, there is more that we can do. Now we have to start gaining a greater understanding of the matter at hand.

So what would this understanding look like? It could be allowing ourselves to register the degree to which the offending parties are disordered and/or emotionally disabled. It can be coming to an understanding that we have given too much credence to others who in actuality have no idea who they are, what goes on inside them, or what drives their actions. It could be coming to understand how affected the offending parties are due to things they have suffered in their own past, thereby helping us get a grasp on the issues they have carried forward. It may also be coming to understand the full impact of their immaturity, character flaws, substance abuse, narcissism, or sociopathic tendencies.

The thing we are attempting to do through this understanding is overturn the belief that whatever occurred took place because of something that we said, did, or are. We are trying to comprehend the situation in a broader sense so that we do not take it personally.

Unfortunately, many of us carry the belief that all life events can be traced directly back to us. There is no consideration of the bigger picture. Everything seems personal. Assuming this to be true, we ply ourselves with self-recriminations. This particular belief is spectacularly wrong. In fact, it is downright outlandish.

Of course, there clearly are things that happen due to our choices and ways of being. We are all busy creating things in this world. This is obvious. However, when interacting with others, we do not have the luxury of creating in a vacuum. We are now in a zone that depends on a plethora of factors, all of which we do not understand or control.

When we interact with others, we are interacting with the following:

- their family history;
- their strength of character or lack of it;
- their defenses;
- their thoughts and thought processes (perceptions/ interpretations, beliefs/convictions, assumptions, expectations, judgments, memories/filters);
- their feelings (both conscious and unconscious);
- their level of maturity;
- their level of narcissism;
- their unresolved issues;
- their fears;
- their biology (genes, hormones, diseases, organ functioning, constitution, blood sugar level, fatigue level, sexuality, general health, etc.);
- their ability or inability to communicate well;
- their emotional hardiness;
- their mental illnesses (mood disorders, developmental disorders, personality disorders, psychoses, perversions, addictions);
- their longings;
- their internal voids;
- their neediness;
- their resistance to growth;
- their chronological age;
- their ability to deal with reality;
- their level of emotional availability;

- their readiness to commit to a relationship;
- their level of awareness;
- their level of impulse control;
- their repetition compulsions;
- their reactions to the effect of weather, planetary movements, solar flares, etc.

We control none of that. Whatever another person is walking around with internally is a wild card for us.

This is not even a complete list. There are so many factors at play within another person that they cannot all be listed here. When you think of all the possibilities and all the potential combinations of factors within another person, it is mind boggling. These are the people whose every word and behavior we take to heart and use to attack ourselves based on their presumed validity. What? Are we crazy?

No, we are not crazy. We probably hold this belief simply because we are lacking in individuation and still hold the perspective that we are connected to every life event. Or perhaps we are partially individuated, but still lack a well-defined sense of self. We do not yet have the strength of our own feelings, our own opinions, our own likes and dislikes, our own ways of being. We are on our way, but still do not have the ego strength to believe in ourselves and to turn aside some of life's absurdities.

Alternatively, we may be engaging in idealization; we may be seeing others to be more aware, mature, and capable than they really are. Or at the very least, we see them as able to be consistently in control of themselves. Then, when something does happen that feels personal, we assume that they did it, not because of their own limitations, but because they did not value us.

The truth is that sometimes others do not know what is going on within us. Nor do they always have control of themselves and their behaviors. They get overloaded, anxious, or depressed and find themselves impulsively acting on their feelings. Even the best of us struggle with maintaining control in stressful situations. This is unfortunate, but it has nothing to do with us.

Worse yet, sometimes we are dealing with more than human limitation; we are dealing with someone who is downright disordered. The damaging behaviors of such individuals are not transient, but in play most of the time. This can be anything from untreated addiction to personality disorders to psychosis. Unfortunately, we are usually unaware of this reality. We assume the other people are normal, and we are shocked and hurt when they do whatever it is that they do. Sometimes we may know about the disorder, but have no real idea of all that their disorder entails. Either scenario is fertile ground for personalization.

An example of this would be dealing with narcissists. People's level of narcissism is a factor in the hurtful things that they say and do. Narcissists are so invested in defending their protective image that they react very poorly to the threat of being unmasked, exposed, or challenged. If threatened, they can lash out with very hurtful comments. If very narcissistic, they do not even know we exist as real, live, four-dimensional individuals who can be hurt by their words and actions. To them we are two-dimensional individuals who exist more as objects to be used. This can lead to exploitive, abusive, and disrespectful behaviors.

If we are facing this without knowledge of the disorder in play, we do not stand a chance in the personalization department. However, if we can acknowledge and register another's disorder, we can reduce or fully eradicate our tendency to take things personally. Once we have done this, it becomes all too clear who has the problem. In these instances, it might even be helpful to ask ourselves the question, "What am I dealing with here?" It can be an eye opener.

When we put all of the above together, it pretty much obliterates the idea that most everything that happens in life is because of us. Really, there is very little that we should take personally. This is not to say that we should not take responsibility for ourselves, but it is to say that our responsibility in any given matter may constitute a very small part of a larger picture.

Now let's switch gears for a moment. So far we have been looking at others' contributions to our taking things personally. However, everything related to personalization is not about the other person. There are certain things that we may be doing that contribute to our tendency to personalize as well. This may seem counterintuitive in that we are trying not to attack ourselves; however, taking responsibility for our own ways of being can rescue us from the painful conviction that someone did something to us because we were not lovable, worthy, or valid. On the contrary, if we can identify a misstep of our own, it can increase our understanding of the matter and actually be very relieving.

In these instances, it can be helpful to remember that taking responsibility does not mean taking blame or being bad. It does not involve a personal judgment so much as an assessment of reality. It is entirely possible to assess reality without pronouncing ourselves worthless, incompetent, stupid, or unlovable.

Let's look at a few possibilities for how we might be a contributing factor in the personalization of our life events. The possibilities listed below are specific, but are all related in some manner to taking responsibility for ourselves.

The first of these is our propensity to engage in self-attack. Do we use this defense regularly? Is it our "go-to" position? We need to take a look and see. In particular, we need to see how we are working with our anger. When someone has done something that is unkind or malicious to us, we can either experience our righteous anger toward the other person or turn it against our self. Turning it against our self will probably result in the hurt of taking things personally. Turning it outwardly against the other person will short-circuit personalization. Of course, this does not mean to outwardly harm someone; it means being appropriately angry with them.

A second thing we have to do when attempting to get past personalization is look at our capacity to set and maintain boundaries for ourselves. Anytime we feel abused, smothered, put upon, used up, manipulated, or disregarded, it is time to set a boundary. We may have to say *no* and mean it, we may have to defend ourselves, or we may have to leave a bad situation. Whatever it is that we need to do, others need to be apprised of where we have no more ground to give. Then they need to see this demonstrated.

Having healthy boundaries means that we are willing to be the protector of our own self rather than assigning that job to someone else. When we assign our self-care to another, we are deep in personalization territory, for when he or she fails to adequately protect us, we will be personally hurt.

When in a relationship we are famous for abdicating our self-care in favor of being cared for by our loved one. This is how we related to our parents when we were children. However, we should never approach another with the boundless innocence of a child, for others are only human and will, at some point, let us down. When they do, we will take it very personally if we have trusted them beyond reason and without bounds. We need to stay realistic.

A third thing we have to look at within ourselves is our level of self-esteem. The less self-esteem we have, the more we tend to take things personally. Another way to say this is that we are more easily hurt when we have lost sight of our worth. We need to be responsible for the fact that when our self-esteem has bottomed out, we are not as emotionally hardy as usual. Taking responsibility for this can make things seem less personal.

A fourth reason we take things personally is that we fail to understand the nature of life. As M. Scott Peck said, "Life is difficult." [1] This is a variation on what the Buddha said: "Life is suffering." [2] Life is not a bowling alley with a varnished pathway to success. It is not a linear passageway affording a straight shot. We can throw a perfect ball all day long and not take down all ten pins. Life is more like a miniature golf course with twists and turns and obstacles everywhere. Life's pathways are winding, frustrating, and full of brambles. It is this way for everyone, not just us. It is the norm. It is the nature of life.

If we can but realize this, we can take life's slings and arrows less personally. We can approach things more philosophically. We can accept the reality that struggle and failure are part of the plan for everybody. It is not just we who try and fail, make the wrong choices, or falter when the burden is too heavy. It is everybody.

When struggling with something difficult or painful in life, it is always helpful to remember that life does not happen *to* us. Nor does life happen to *us*. Life just happens. Remembering this will lift us out of personalization very quickly.

A fifth thing we need to do in order to stop taking things personally is to admit when one of our own issues or disorders is in play. For instance, sometimes we are the narcissistic ones who demand such special treatment that no one is allowed to criticize or disagree with us at all. We are so fragile inside that no one dare speak to us unless it is to admire us and support our thoughts, feelings, and choices. From this vantage point, pretty much everything that is not approving and admiring is felt to be a personal attack. Moreover, every little thing that we thought we should receive but did not is experienced as a slight and wounds us greatly.

Obviously, we cannot be in the position to dictate what others may do or say to constantly protect our egos. In such instances, we need a couple of things. We need a stronger sense of self, i.e., have a greater awareness and appreciation of who we are as individuals. In addition, we need more compassion for the actual self and less emphasis on the idealized self. Once we are more defined as individuals and accepting of our actual self, every difference of opinion or aberrant behavior will not feel like a personal attack upon us.

A sixth thing we need to do to minimize personalization is to be aware of how we are interpreting our environment, for we can concoct some pretty self-denigrating stories about why someone out in the world did or said whatever he or she did. If we are to avoid taking things personally, we cannot be our own worst enemies when it comes to seeing things clearly. We may not like what we see, but it is better than twisting incoming information into denigrating, self-attacking sagas about how unloved and unimportant we are.

A seventh thing we need to do in order to minimize personalization is to come to a compassionate understanding of the behaviors we have engaged in and the life choices we have made. Understanding and compassion always help.

Here are a few possibilities for why we might have behaved badly or chosen poorly:

- Maybe we did whatever we did because we were unusually needy or simply naïve.
- Maybe we were attracted to what felt familiar from our family of origin (even if what felt familiar was hurtful); in our minds, home equals love no matter what home was actually like.
- Maybe our fears got in the way of our self-care.
- Maybe we projected our goodness onto an undeserving person.
- Maybe we erroneously thought that we would get back what we put in, not realizing that we do not control the universe with our goodness. Sometimes our goodness is not even seen, able to be received, or is interpreted incorrectly.
- Maybe we had no way of knowing the psychological issues at work within another.
- Maybe we thought we deserved punishment.
- Maybe we wanted to feel special and worthwhile by rescuing someone who needed saving, but that person could not be saved without his or her own efforts.

- Maybe we failed to see that our efforts to help another amounted to an attempt to control.
- Maybe we chose a person who was weak so we could not be controlled by him or her.
- Maybe we chose someone who was needy so that he or she would not leave us.
- Maybe we were too dependent.
- Maybe we had not developed ourselves sufficiently to be able to safely relate without losing ourselves in the process.

There are so many possibilities for why we do what we do, but none of them should be cause for self-flagellation. Nor should they be misconstrued as the singular reason that certain things happen (particularly in relationships). Whatever another person says or does, it does not mean that his or her actions have been completely predicated upon our choices and behaviors. The workings of relationships are far more complex than that. We can take responsibility for our part in a matter without exaggerating it in such an absurd manner. The best thing we can do is to learn about ourselves from our mistakes and recognize that the other person has a lot to acknowledge as well. It is important that we learn to accept not only our own foibles, but those of others as well.

Oftentimes our choices, behaviors, and ways of being are unconscious ones. In fact, we may have no idea what is motivating us. When we come to the realization that many of our regrettable behaviors have arisen out of unconsciousness, we can begin to forgive ourselves. If we choose to do this, letting in the knowledge that our unconscious behaviors are not our fault, there may be a feeling of relief, gratitude, and humility. We may feel merciful toward ourselves. We may even vow to work on becoming more conscious human beings. In fact, our awareness of the reality that we have been unconscious has already moved us forward in the awareness department. This brings us confidence in our ability to achieve better connections with others and to improve the quality of our lives.

As we come to realize that we cannot hold ourselves responsible for choices and behaviors that are born of unconsciousness, it becomes clear that we cannot hold others responsible for their unconscious choices and behaviors either. Granted, we may have to remove ourselves from certain situations if those choices and behaviors become too unhealthy for us, but we do not have to view other people's actions as conscious attempts to hurt us. This realization can help us take things less personally. Specifically, it can help us release the idea that we are being personally targeted and/or punished by others.

An eighth thing we can do to minimize personalization is to give up our victim status. This means that we have to relinquish the idea that we are innocent, hapless bystanders in life who, for some unexplainable reason, keep getting run over. However, that presents a problem because being a victim provides many perks. Victims are innocent. Victims are not responsible for anything that happens. In fact, they are absolved of all responsibility. They have no need for remorse. Victims are perceived to be the good ones, not the bad ones. They are loveable and worthwhile, wounded by circumstances, and nothing can be held against them. It is easy to see how we might be very attached to our victim status.

Without our victim status we would have to contend openly with our responsibility to self and others. We would have to own our self-attack. We would have to face our lack of compassion to self. We would have to confront our fears about our own worth and lovability. We might even have to admit that we have had a contribution to the matter at hand. These are the things we are trying to avoid by holding on to our unrelenting judgment of others while relishing the conviction of our own victimhood. Yet in reality it is our identification with being a victim and holding on to the feeling of being wronged that exacerbates our feelings of worthlessness, lack of lovability, badness, guilt, and shame.

Without our judgment of others and without the victim mask to hide behind, there is a calm that descends. We cease to see ourselves as slaughtered innocents and begin to see ourselves as normal human beings dealing with one of life's curve balls. We feel less angry and helpless as we reclaim our own power to cope; consequently, there is less vitriol to turn back on ourselves. We also feel less sanctimonious as we begin to look at our possible part in the matter at hand (even if our part was no more than allowing certain persons into our lives). If there is not partial responsibility for us to declare, then at least we can claim our power to heal and once again find joy in life.

Go ahead and try it on for size. Think of someone you do not like and cannot forgive. Note how you feel like a victim of his/her behaviors. Then note what it would feel like if you had to give up your victim status. What would you have to relinquish? Do you see how you would have to give up your powerlessness? Do you see how you would have to abandon your focus on the other person and take a look at how you are processing your emotions? Do you see how it is your own self-attack that has left you feeling depressed and personally flawed? If so, you would come to realize that you were never be a victim to begin with. You were just someone who misdirected your rage, gave your power away, and then suffered the consequences of that. Do you see the difference in how you feel?

Giving up our victimhood does not mean that now we realize nothing bad has really happened to us or that now we realize what has happened is our fault. Nor does it not mean that we are expected to have no negative feelings about what has happened. On the contrary, we will have grief that we need to process. It is just that we will be minus the self-attack component of the offense or at least it will be lowered. The conviction of our victimhood has only been there to supposedly help us reclaim our goodness, our worth, our lovability, our validity, and our innocence. It has been a failing attempt to get us out of pain, which inadvertently has caused more pain.

The relinquishment of our victim consciousness shows us what we were struggling with at the outset – not the offender, but our own self-attack. It allows for a compassionate response to our loss of lovability, validity, innocence, worth, and goodness. It sheds the light of loving understanding on them. It embraces them. More than that, it takes the power away from the offender and restores it to us. We begin to see that these questions about our own value should never have been entertained. We were valuable to begin with. We see that more of our pain has been due to the questioning of our own worth, goodness, and lovability than to any action of the perpetrator. He or she just got us doubting ourselves. It is much easier to take a loss when we know we are loveable, good, and worthy.

The restoration of power that occurs within us when we realize our own worth brings an amazing release because the offending party has now lost power over us and that person knows it. He or she may have had us on the run for a while, but all that is over now, for as soon as we stop beating on ourselves, the offender's ability to beat on us vanishes as well. It is amazing how when we forgive ourselves for our real or imagined flaws, everything turns around. Whether we see it as the best way to get our revenge, the best way to forgive other lost souls, or the best way to find our own peace of mind, our power lies in letting ourselves off the hook.

So if we are not victims, what are we? We may be individuals who have had to put up with something, we may be individuals with limited awareness, or we may be naïve individuals. We may be individuals who are sometimes driven by our historical issues or our fears or our low self-esteem. We may be individuals with less than a perfect grasp of a situation, with limited knowledge of a particular subject, or limited power to handle a situation as we would have liked. We may be imperfect perceivers of a given situation. We may even be brainwashed individuals. However, we are rarely bad individuals. We are simply fallible human beings doing the best we can.

You may ask, "What about the times when children are harmed or have an illness and they really are victims? Or what about the times we adults are the victims of crimes? What about people who are victimized by terrorists?

To this we can say that of course there are situations in which we are powerless against forces around us. At these times, yes, we can acknowledge that we have been victimized. We definitely have losses to deal with. But this is very different from victim consciousness which singlehandedly reduces our own power and seeks further victimization in order to keep repetitively proving to the world that we are good. We can be the victim of someone or something, see it as part of living on planet earth, meet it with grace, and move on without seeking our own redemption through a pattern of victim consciousness.

Ninth, if we are to give up personalization, we must embrace the concept of acceptance. This means that we must stop fighting against life. We have to stop arguing with reality and agree to accept it. We have to stop carrying on about whether or not something was right or fair and instead jump straight to what needs to be done, given the reality that presents itself. After we have processed our initial emotions and tried to gain an understanding of the situation, we must always say to ourselves, "This is my reality. Now what do people with this reality do?"

At this point, all judgments against self or others are useless. They simply get in the way of accepting reality, finding solutions to deal with that reality, and eventually achieving forgiveness for all concerned.

The concept of acceptance does not demand that we pretend whatever happened did not actually happen. That would be a denial of truth and constitute lying to ourselves. We do not want to associate forgiveness with lying. But we need to understand that *what is* **is** and that it is our label of our life experience as good or bad that presents a problem. We simply need to overlook the judgment piece and get to a reality-based, healing solution.

This reality-based, healing solution could be:

- starting over;
- redirecting our interests elsewhere;
- making new choices;
- relating on a less trusting and/or intimate basis;
- taking charge of our own finances;
- making realistic assessments of another's true abilities;
- becoming more independent;
- being less gullible;
- setting more boundaries for ourselves;
- getting out of denial;
- educating ourselves about addiction or abuse and registering what we are learning.

A tenth thing that contributes to personalization is a lack of communication with the offender. Sometimes communication with the offender is not possible, but when it is, it can be a glorious redeemer of our worth. Through communication, we take in new information that can help us view the situation in a more understandable light. We can calm down, stop assuming the worst about ourselves, and get on with things.

In a best-case scenario in which both parties are working to resolve the situation, the understanding we need can be gleaned through direct communication that clears up misperceptions and misunderstandings. Healing can go forward much more easily when the offender and the wounded party are both talking. It can also go forward when the offender admits to his or her offense and seeks help to achieve a greater understanding of him- or herself. Hit-and-run offenses are the worst-case scenarios. The injured party is left with the worst thoughts about him- or herself with no way to know why the injurious event occurred. Here self-attack can run rampant.

When the offending party is not ready or willing to admit to his or her offense, however, it is useless to try to achieve healing through interaction with that person. That would amount to the useless pastime of trying to change someone. That would be waiting to be heard by someone who is not listening. That would be codependency. In these instances the healing must be internal and the focus must be on self.

The hardest internal or external judgment to let go of is when the offending party did something on purpose. They knew exactly what they were doing. Maybe they were downright evil. It gets very personal here because there is less possibility for innocence (theirs and ours). The offender seems unusually heartless and we seem unusually worthless.

Yet in reality, persons who are willfully harming others are usually the ones who know least what they are really doing. Oh sure, they dimly know they are slashing and burning other people, but they are unusually lacking in awareness of themselves, of their motivations, of others, or of the effects of their actions. They are so lost in their own hostility, their own issues, and their own fears that they could not find their way out of a paper bag. They know practically nothing about themselves. Worse, the actions they engage in completely block their ability to feel anything, for action blocks awareness of emotion. In fact, they are such ignorant messes that truly we can only forgive them for they know not what they do.

The reality is that almost nothing that happens is personal. It may seem personal, but it is not. Even when something negative or hurtful is directed at us, it is largely due to the inner state of the offender; the more outrageous the offense, the more disturbed the offender. No matter how specifically directed an action is against us, it is not about us. Were we perfect in the matter? Probably not. Did we have our own issues that came into play? Probably. Does that have anything to do with deserving a beating? No, definitely not.

When we find that we are unable to relinquish a judgment of another and are simultaneously attacking ourselves, it is helpful to take a look at what the judgment is doing for us. We might try asking ourselves the following questions:

- Am I holding on to my judgment to establish that I am right? Does this help me to confirm that the problem is someone else's?
- Am I holding on to my judgment in an attempt to feel more powerful and in control? Does it help me feel reassured that I won't be controlled or taken over by another person?
- Am I holding on to my judgment in an attempt to feel like the good one? Am I holding on to my judgment to help me feel innocent and/or absolve myself of guilt?
- Am I holding on to my judgment to make the offender feel guilty or ashamed?
- Am I punishing the offender with my unwillingness to forgive? If so, how is this going to help me meet my goals for the relationship?
- Am I holding on to my judgment to protect myself from being hurt again? Does the distance it creates help me feel safe? Is this position of judgment better than being emotionally vulnerable?
- Is holding on to my judgment the only way I can set boundaries for myself? Is holding on to my judgment the only way I can engage in self-care?
- Am I holding on to my judgment to help myself avoid taking responsibility for my own choices?
- Am I holding on to my judgment to help myself feel motivated to make a change? Is it the only way to leave a relationship?
- Am I holding on to my judgment to help myself remain in a relationship through involvement, drama, and emotional intensity? Does it help me remain emotionally connected to another even when things appear to be over?
- Am I holding on to my judgment because my ego is involved? Is there a pride position at stake? Am I finding it difficult to humbly admit my deficiencies?

- Am I holding on to my judgment to fuel a social or political cause rather than address it as a personal issue?
- Am I holding on to my judgment because I have not spoken out and/or stood up for myself? Am I angry with myself for my lack of assertion?
- Does my unwillingness to forgive indicate that I'm engaged in a power struggle? How is this better than heartfelt communication?
- Does refusing to forgive help me avoid feeling like a failure? Does it help me avoid feeling stupid or worthless? Does it help me avoid feeling disappointed, sad, afraid, or helpless?
- Is my inability to forgive a person in my present tied to my grief or anger about someone in my past?
- Is my inability to forgive tied to helping me remain a victim?
- Am I unable to forgive because I think I should have known better?
- If I forgive, will I drop into the background and never be heard again? Is staying in an unforgiving position the only way I can be heard?
- Do I hold judgments as a method of communication rather than communicating directly? Is holding a grudge the only way I can make my point?
- Is my inability to forgive related to shock and disbelief about something that has happened?
- Do I feel like I can't forgive because others have refused to support my position?
- Do I feel like I can't forgive because I will feel like I am betraying my emotional self? Is holding on to my wounds the only way that I can honor my emotions?
- Do I fear that if I forgive, I will appear weak? Am I afraid that if I forgive, I will not be taken seriously?
- Am I holding on to my judgment to defend myself against intimately relating to others? Does holding on

to my judgment allow me to avoid commitment? Does it allow me to remain distant and uninvolved in my relationships?

Whether we are answering these questions so that we can forgive ourselves or forgive another, they are worthy of our attention. They shift our focus inward to the self, which moves us closer to understanding and benevolence for all.

Chapter 20

ANXIETY AND SELF-ATTACK

Although anxiety can arise from a variety of sources, it is being included in the section of this book that focuses on self-attack. This is because some anxiety is a direct result of self-attack and some, although indirectly related, generates a painful onslaught to the self that is an assault in its own right.

Anxiety is an emotional state that is characterized by excessive worry, uneasiness, uncertainty, and apprehension. It is partially a physiological phenomenon and partly a psychological one. It is physiological in that it involves disturbed breathing, increased heart activity, vasomotor changes (sweating, flushing), and musculoskeletal disturbances (trembling, paralysis). It is psychological in that it involves an emotional state characterized by the following: [1]

- a feeling of powerlessness to do anything about a particular matter;
- a feeling of foreboding that danger is impending and almost inevitable;
- a tense, exhausting state of alertness;
- an apprehensive self-absorption that stands in the way of effective problem solving;
- an irresolvable doubt about the nature of the upcoming danger;

- an irresolvable doubt about the probability that the upcoming danger will emerge;
- an irresolvable doubt over the best way to reduce or eradicate the upcoming danger;
- an irresolvable doubt about whether or not one has the personal capacity to reduce or eradicate the upcoming danger.

Anxiety is different from fear, which lacks the fourth and fifth characteristics on the list above. Anxiety is typically more about danger that is unreal, imagined, or undefined, thereby interfering with problem solving. Fear is about a real, defined, threatening danger which lends itself more to problem solving.

In managing anxiety it can be very helpful to determine whether or not our apprehensive feeling is indeed about something real or if our minds are simply playing tricks on us. If our feeling turns out to be about something real, then we can identify it as a bona fide fear. This allows us to ascertain the upcoming threat, learn about it as much as possible, strategize to determine upcoming moves and countermoves, and shore up our areas of weakness. In other words, we can prepare a plan. All of this can give us a better sense of control, minimize our self-absorbed obsessing, and open the door to effective problem solving.

Facing a legitimate fear grants us access to our warrior mode. In this mode we can take charge and do whatever is necessary to prepare for the battle. It is an active, preparatory mode that does not intend to let us be sitting ducks. It can be something simple like taking a prep course to correct an area of deficiency, studying or practicing diligently, hurricane preparedness, or rehearsing a speech. It might be something complex like working with an attorney about a lawsuit, overhauling a business plan, or preparing a military strategy. Whatever the case, it involves full acknowledgment of the problem, thoughtful planning, and then corrective or defensive action.

Anxiety is a tougher nut to crack than fear because we do not know what to prepare for, and even if we did know, we are too busy obsessing to do anything about it. To make matters worse, our minds can convince us of almost anything. However, it is possible to start getting a handle on our anxiety if we can determine where it is originating. Once we know where it is originating, we can get to work in the right area. To this end, here is a list below of ten areas in which anxiety can originate.

The first area to be considered has to do with one of our earliest stages of development. Specifically, it has to do with whether or not we have matured beyond the symbiotic stage with our primary love objects (usually our parents) and moved on to create a separate sense of self. When we have developed a separate sense of self, this is called individuation. If we have not individuated sufficiently to create a separate self, we remain dependent, and dependency can be a major source of anxiety.

The more dependent we are, the more anxious we tend to be. This is because when we are dependent on someone, we are at that person's mercy. We are reliant on that person's awareness, attunement, and good will to supply us with our need fulfillment. This sort of situation can be unusually bad when the other person is self-absorbed, addicted, ill-equipped, naïve, mentally ill, unpredictable, untrustworthy, lacking in resources, etc.

It can be tempting to remain merged with our original love objects, for this can be a comforting place, but it can also be a frightening place as it affords us no sovereignty and no control over our own lives. This lack of control fuels anxiety. We need the autonomy individuation provides so that we can be self-governing and make the best choices for our self.

This does not mean that we should develop an exaggerated sense of independence in which we eschew any sort of reliance on another. We can take pleasure in having another to rely on. It is simply to say that reliance on someone else cannot be our only source of strength. We should always have our own strengths in place so that we can take care of our own needs.

When taking stock of our level of dependency, it is important to be aware of the fact that we all have dependency needs. These include our basic needs for safety, nourishment, shelter, love, and connection. We should not berate ourselves for having them. It is only when we find ourselves depending too much on others to fulfill these needs that we should be concerned.

Over-reliance on others is a big generator of separation anxiety, the fear of being separated from our caregiver or home. It is characterized by a dread of deprivation and/or death. It can be terrorizing for the unindividuated person. However, the more we are able to develop a separate sense of self, the better able we are to care for ourselves and thus experience less anxiety about our own survival.

Individuation takes place gradually and in stages; it is not an either/or thing. Thus we may be independent in some areas and remain dependent in others. Perhaps we have become aware of our own likes and dislikes, our own opinions, and our own feelings, but are not yet able to stand firm on certain issues.

In order to lessen our anxiety, we need to individuate to the point that we have developed the ability to resolutely say *no*, i.e., to set personal boundaries for ourselves. If we do not have our boundaries in place, anybody can do anything to us because we have no means to stop him or her. We do not have limits. We do not have a line over which others may not cross.

It has been said that being in this state is like being in a room that has a door on either side. There are doorknobs on the outside of both doors. Anybody can come or go from the outside and do anything to us he or she wants. However, there are no door knobs on the inside. There is no way for us to leave. We must stay and put up with whatever happens.

If we want to stay out of such a place, we must determine where we have no more ground to give and then follow it up. We do not wait for others to hear us or understand us or stop what they are doing. We set a limit for *our self*. We do whatever we have to do to make our lives better. We stop rescuing others. We do not enable addiction. We do not put up with abuse. We figure out how to make our own way. We may even have to leave.

Lack of individuation and the limited or nonexistent personal boundaries that accompany it can give rise to a deep anxiety about relating closely to others; we can become downright avoidant regarding emotional intimacy and commitment. The dynamic here is that if we merge with another without a strong sense of self, we will not be able to reemerge intact. There is the thought that we will somehow end up being controlled, devoured, used, abused, or discounted. We will lose all of our ability to stand firm as individuals and be swept away, or we will be relegated to being satellites that merely orbit the main planet (the person with whom we are merged). All in all, closeness and intimacy are a dangerous proposition for us.

Fear of merger can be a particular danger for us when we are feeling especially needy and know that we will most likely put up with more than we should. Our need will overpower our resolution to maintain self-care. We will do too much, give too much, love too much, and not speak up enough. It can be a tough call when we are finally getting some of our needs met, yet if we do not stand up for ourselves, we will end up consistently fearing our loved ones as much as we care about them. Worse yet, we may not be able to forge close relationships at all.

A second cause of anxiety is repressed anger or repressed grief. When these feelings reside outside of our awareness, they can cause or contribute to panic attacks, obsessive-compulsive behaviors, phobias, hoarding, and generalized anxiety to name a few. The outrage and/or anguish that we carry unbeknownst to us makes us shake, quiver, worry, and obsess. Sometimes it makes us feel like we cannot breathe and are going to die. Our feelings of anger and grief are trying very hard to enter our consciousness where they can be acknowledged, understood, and released, but until this occurs, we will continue to have anxiety symptoms.

We all know what it is like to be full of acknowledged outrage about an event or interaction (almost to the point that we are trembling) and then later experience the deep relief and relaxation of having verbalized our fury and gotten it all out. This is a similar dynamic to that of releasing repressed anger and/or grief, only here we first have to acknowledge that there is something present to be gotten out. Unfortunately, as long as repression (a form of forgetting) is in play, whatever we need to express will remain out of our consciousness and therefore cannot find expression.

Unexpressed anger and grief are not only present in painful situations that we refuse to acknowledge. Sometimes when there has been a painful loss or upsetting event, we can intellectually acknowledge it or even acknowledge the feelings involved, but we are not yet able to tolerate experiencing those feelings. Instead, we think about our losses and the feelings that may accompany them in a detached manner. Here we are not repressing our feelings, but we are defending against our feelings through the use of intellect, which can result in symptoms of anxiety. In these cases of intellectualization, anxiety will be present because of all the anger and grief that has not yet been experienced and expressed. Enforced losses such as death, loss of a job, or loss of a relationship entail so much loss of attachment, so much grief, and so much anger that it can take time to process it all. When we do get through processing it, however, our anxiety will abate.

We can find blessed relief from these anxiety disorders if we simply get honest with ourselves about how a given situation or relationship is impacting us. This can be very difficult to do when the stakes are high (marriage, job, death, etc.). Much of the time we do not let ourselves know just how upset and/or unhappy with really are. We want to protect the status quo, yet as long as we do not challenge it (if only within ourselves), our dishonesty will cause us deep anxiety.

A third cause of anxiety is sexual longing that cannot find expression. This is present not just because a biological urge has been thwarted, but also because there can be a sense of helplessness, loneliness, depression, and self-loathing that accompanies the inability to find an appropriate partner.

Inevitably there is tremendous anger, bitterness, and heartache that sets in if the situation does not improve. When not processed correctly, all this can result in anxiety.

In situations like this the use of sublimation can be helpful. This is when we direct our energies into other areas that may not be as fully satisfying as sexual contact, but can provide satisfaction to a large degree. This can be any activity that we love to engage in or that leaves us feeling connected to something meaningful. It is a redirection of our creative sexual energy to other creative endeavors.

Of course, in such cases there should also be a shoring up of social skills as well as an exploration of several issues such as fear of intimacy, fear of commitment, self-sabotaging tendencies, religious dictates, fear of failure, or impeding personality traits.

A fourth cause of anxiety is when the psyche is overwhelmed by too great an influx of stimuli that cannot be discharged or mastered. [2] This can be stimuli originating from either within or without. If it is a stimulus originating from within, this is usually coming from the id (the fully unconscious part of the psychic apparatus that is unrestrained in its drives). Since the id works on the pleasure principle, it is constantly urging us to engage in whatever would satiate us at the moment without regard for the conscious self that would like to make more appropriate choices. This can be conflictual and overwhelming at times, but if we have a kindhearted understanding of the nature of the id and a good grasp on the choices we consciously want to make, it should not present too much of a problem.

If too many anxiety-producing stimuli are originating from the outer world rather than our inner world, we are obligated to reconsider our external environment. Perhaps we need to change what we are exposing ourselves to whether that involves changing friends, changing our relationship status, changing our work environment, or changing our forms of entertainment. There are so many ways that we can reduce our exposure to irritating stimuli even if it is as simple as putting our phones down. We can also surround ourselves with soothing colors, listen to soothing music, pare down our to-do lists, turn off the television, and stop following the daily news. The possibilities are endless.

A fifth source of anxiety is the superego (the part of our psychic apparatus that acts as a judge, arbiter of right and wrong, the conscience). This part of us is the voice of our parents, teachers, religious figures, and society that we have taken in as our own. It dictates if we have or have not erred and punishes us if it thinks we have. It demands that we make amends for what we have supposedly done. Its favorite thing to do is to punish us with guilt or shame, which results in a loss of self-esteem.

The superego can be extremely punitive or rather benign depending on how the voices of our parents, teachers, religious figures, and society came to us in our youth. If they were harsh, our superegos will be critical and unforgiving. If they were kind and understanding, our superegos will be benevolent and altruistic. Unfortunately, many of us have rather harsh superegos and as a result, carry around a good deal of anxiety over whatever punitive pronouncements and severe punishments may come at any time.

It can be very difficult to carry around an abusive inner law enforcement official who seems to be looking for our every infraction. Self-attack can run rampant with this dynamic in play. Here it becomes very important to see the superego for exactly what it is, the hypercritical voice of people who knew little to nothing about compassion and self-love. Once we understand this, we can discount much of what it has to say, retaining only that which we deem reasonable. This alone will reduce our anxiety and keep our self-esteem bolstered.

Once again, the observing self comes to our rescue as we stand apart from the superego and observe its behaviors in a dispassionate way. Once we have surveyed the superego and taken notes, we can make our own moves to protect ourselves from self-punishment, thus keeping our anxiety to tolerable levels.

A sixth source of anxiety is the gap between the idealized self and the actual self. This leads to the pursuit of unrealistic goals, impossible standards of perfection, and absurd expectations. This subject has already been covered at length earlier in the book, but suffice it to say that the more we demand of ourselves and the less we acknowledge being human, the higher our anxiety level will be.

Moreover, by holding superhuman standards for ourselves, we relegate ourselves to continually having to protect our overinflated, narcissistic image, hoping against hope that no one will be able to unmask us. We live in the secret fear that someone may come along and see the truth: that we do not actually have perfect control of everything in our lives. They might also see that we are secretly weak and empty and in need of constant bolstering. In substituting an image for a real self, we also relegate ourselves to never achieving true fulfillment, since pouring our efforts into an image cannot provide fulfillment. Only nourishment of the actual self can provide that.

A seventh cause for anxiety is when we anticipate the recurrence of a traumatic situation that has taken place in the past; we become anxiously hypervigilant, girding ourselves ahead of time in the event that the original trauma may recur. This sort of preventive readiness is sometimes called signal anxiety and is learned in the course of our childhood development. Perhaps we are anticipating a lack of sensitivity, connection, and need fulfillment. Perhaps we are expecting abandonment, disapproval, emotional withdrawal, erratic behavior, or punishment. The list is long.

Generally speaking, however, in our earliest, most dependent stage of development, anticipatory anxiety is usually centered around the potential loss of a life-sustaining love object (separation anxiety). When we are a bit older, our anxiety centers not around the possibility that we cannot live without our love object(s), but the possibility of the loss of their love, particularly if we do not perform up to their standards. Later on our anticipatory anxiety revolves around a fear of punishment, particularly if there is competition for the affections of our love object. This is sometimes termed castration anxiety. After that our anticipatory anxiety becomes more internal than external as we come to anticipate the wrath of our own superego.

All of these possibilities for anxiety involve leaving our present moment as we move into an anticipatory mode. It is best to remain squarely present as much as possible in order to counter this movement into the future. In order to stay present, we can employ the use of breathing techniques, pay close attention to our sensory experience of the present moment, or be mindful of each thing that comprises our present moment. We can also use our power of observation to note that we are beginning to tense up and that there is no threatening stimulus on the horizon. We can also do some family of origin work (work on issues regarding our biological or adoptive family) in which we process some of our childhood traumas so that they do not remain fully charged and present such an ongoing danger to us.

An eighth source of anxiety is a lack of control of our inner and/or outer environment. Usually these two are connected, for when our external environment is out of control, we tend to become inwardly out of control. Once our inner environment gets out of control, we feel like we are fragmenting or disintegrating, which is tremendously frightening to us. We become deeply alarmed over the possibility of not having our needs met. We dread not having options and choices. We are terrified that we cannot function as we normally do. We cannot concentrate, think rationally, remember anything, complete tasks, or make effective decisions. Perhaps all we can do is cry or shake or curl up in a ball while we await annihilation. We certainly cannot make our way in life as we once did.

Once things become this bad, medication is usually indicated along with a serious course of therapy. The medication helps stabilize us so we can start getting a handle on how to problem-solve whatever is going on within our lives. It also gives us the opportunity to determine whether or not our decompensated state (nonfunctional state) has more to do with how we are attacking our self or with whatever is happening in our outer environment. Eventually we can devise a plan of action and carry it through. If losses are involved, we will probably have a lot of anger and grief to process, and we will need to work with the concept of acceptance. We will also have to reconnect to our own strengths. We may even have to reinvent ourselves or construct an entirely new way of life.

If we are not terribly decompensated, all of this can be done without medication. It is just a matter of getting ahead of our morbid ruminations by separating ourselves from them through observation. Then we can effectively see them and challenge them. It is about confronting ourselves to think about things differently, perceive things differently, and a refusal to succumb to hopelessness. In other words, it is about our willingness to tell ourselves a different story rather than the despairing one we have thus far told ourselves. As always, we must first do the inner work of processing our feelings, but after that it is vital that we pay close attention to whether or not we are using our thought processes to our detriment or our advantage.

Anxiety about a lack of control is usually connected to fear of loss. We may be losing our house, our job, our relationship, our financial solvency, our youth, our relevancy, or our health, to name a few. All are deeply terrorizing. However, once we have fought the good fight and done whatever we can to forestall our losses, we must work to embrace reality rather than continue to fight against it. Once the milk is spilt, it cannot be gotten back. This recognition of the futility of struggle against the inevitable will help us stop needlessly thrashing about.

We may not be able to stem the tide of loss or bring back that which is already lost, but we do have control of how we deal with our losses. We do control our self-talk, our attitudes, our level of self-care, our observation of self, our thoughts, our interpretations, our appreciation of things that remain, our spiritual practices, our level of humility, our unrealistic expectations, our degree of patience, and our efforts to rebuild. In these regards we have much that we still can either control or influence. It is simply that these areas of control reside within rather than without.

Whenever there is loss, there is also the need for adjustment. How we adjust or fight against adjustment determines our stress levels and our psychological and physiological states. Sometimes it is easier to adjust to a given situation than it is at other times depending on how fatigued we are and how emotionally burdened we are from the presence of multiple stressors or prolonged stressors. When we do have multiple or prolonged stressors, we must be particularly kind to ourselves as we attempt to grieve our losses and adapt to our new reality. In this process, it is of the utmost importance that we not succumb to illusions of superhuman functioning. We do not need self-attack on top of all that has happened to begin with. Truly, there is no one who controls the universe, no matter how good, how spiritual, how loving, how smart, or how competent he or she is.

A ninth source of anxiety has to do with the displacement of unacceptable impulses (usually sexual or aggressive impulses) onto an external object. This external object symbolically represents either a temptation generated by a forbidden impulse or a punishment for this temptation. The object here is to get rid of our supposedly unacceptable impulses by transferring them elsewhere outside the self. However, this does not work, as the emotional charge that was once attached to our inner impulse is now attached to the external object. As a result, we now proceed to react to the external object with high anxiety, dread, and avoidance. Voilà! A phobia has been born.

Here are a few examples of phobias arising from our forbidden, aggressive impulses. Let's assume that we have high levels of unacceptable rage toward our partners, who are abusive. At times we wish that we could get rid of them. This is a tempting but unacceptable impulse, so instead of acknowledging it and choosing to keep our behaviors in check, we may project our aggressive impulses onto a symbolic object that could "maim" or "murder" these offending parties. This could be broken glass, knives, or firearms. It could be pillows for smothering them, windows to throw them out of, rope for strangling them, a car to run them over, or big animals to attack them. The homicidal possibilities are endless. Whatever we end up choosing as a symbolic representation of our aggressive impulses will be deeply feared and avoided.

It must be said that our aggressive impulses, which we are so keen to disown, are usually temporary and have no serious basis in reality. When we speak of "murderous" impulses or a wish to "get rid" of someone, we are not really going to kill or get rid of that person. We may want to send an offending party to the moon for a while or feel for a moment that we can wring his or her neck. We may even want to "cartoon" kill the wrongdoer where he or she pops right back up, but that is about it. So all this displacing of "unacceptable" impulses is quite unnecessary. It is only seething, long-held, unacknowledged or unexpressed rage that is a danger.

In cases where we have had the urge to "kill," self-punishment is usually close on its heels. In fact, death phobias can arise as a punishment for having had "death" wishes for another. Perhaps we do not wish to "kill" someone, but just injure that person. In these instances we may develop a phobia tied to anything that can injure us.

The displacement of aggressive impulses primarily aimed toward our self can also result in a phobia. For instance, if we feel suicidal, we may displace our self-attacking impulses onto bridges from which we might fall, horses that might trample us, water that may drown us, or ski lifts from which we might plunge.

When our unacceptable impulses have to do with our sexual drive, we manage to displace them onto symbolic objects that terrorize us in exactly the same way as do our aggressive drives. Here are a few examples of phobias that are generated by our forbidden sexual impulses. Our passionate, "animal-like" sexual drive may be represented as a phobia of small creatures such as insects, spiders, and snakes. A fear of touching things like a doorknob that is believed to be dirty can represent our fear of touching ourselves (masturbation) or touching others (sexual contact). A phobia of dirty restrooms can also represent erotic temptations that we believe to be "dirty" temptations.

Not all phobias involve unacceptable drives and impulses. They may have less extreme underpinnings and simply represent a disowned feeling that we carry. However, they will still involve symbolic displacement. For example, if we feel like we have been deeply controlled, truncated, and cut off from every avenue we wish to pursue, we may feel mutilated in some way, as if we have had valuable parts of ourselves disallowed or excised. If we need to avoid awareness of the fact that we feel mutilated or dismembered, we may displace these feelings on amputees who will now symbolically represent our own feelings of dismemberment and mutilation. Then we will feel deep, phobic anxiety and a wish to elude amputees.

If we feel deeply consumed (used up or taken over) by the demands of another individual, we may develop a phobia symbolizing being consumed or eaten up, such as a cancer phobia. This fear of consumption also could result in a phobia about impregnation, being poisoned, or being infected. If we are dealing with demanding children, needy spouses, overly involved parents, or insistent bosses, all of whom devour us, we may also develop an unreasonable fear of anything that can take us over such as doctors, hospitals, needy people, intimate relationships, sloppy kisses, sick people, or big breasts.

If we feel out of control, vulnerable, and powerless, we may become phobic about flying since only the pilot is in control during flight. If we feel overly regulated, restricted, or trapped, we may become phobic about tight clothes, close quarters, elevators, or demanding authority figures. If we feel weak, defenseless, or marginalized, we may become phobic about aged individuals or homeless individuals.

Obviously, some of these phobias are easier to trace back to their source than others, but whatever the case, the remedy for our phobias is to reel our feelings back into ourselves and fully claim them. Nothing within us is so unacceptable that we cannot face it. In fact, much within us could be healed if we would face our original feelings and impulses. If we can do this, then an important part of ourselves will become known, welcomed, and integrated as a vital part of self.

A tenth source of anxiety is negative self-talk. Self-talk refers to the way that we are inwardly talking to ourselves. Negative self-talk occurs when we speak to ourselves in a disparaging way. Our self-talk is related to the kind of thoughts that we hold and the way that we interpret our environment. We can hold dreary, frightful thoughts that generate dreary, frightful messages to ourselves. Likewise, we can hold courageous, supportive thoughts that generate messages of self-confidence, bravery, and encouragement. It all comes down to what kind of story we are telling ourselves.

Unfortunately, the emotional self recognizes our voice and believes everything we say. It is already immature, vulnerable, and sensitive, and does not respond well to horror stories about what terrible things are probably going to happen to it. It does not need to hear catastrophic statements. It does not need to hear that the sky is falling and we are all going to die. This is totally counterproductive and unacceptable.

Even though we may not think we are speaking to ourselves in this manner, if we notice that we are experiencing a high level of readiness brought about by high levels of adrenaline within our bodies, we most likely are. Anxiety is simply adrenaline coursing through our bodies, readying us to either fight or take flight based on the information we are giving our emotional self. When we notice an adrenalized state within our bodies, we must immediately look to see what kind of inner messaging is occurring.

Rather than terrorize the emotional self, we need to support it. It will support us, if we will support it. If we do not support it, it can run amok and deluge us with overwhelming anxiety. When the emotional self gets anxious about one thing or another, it is our job to soothe it as we would a child; our self-talk needs to be calming, encouraging, and reassuring. We might also choose to make pronouncements of a positive nature. We can tell it strongly what we intend to do, how we will execute our plan, and how we will prevail.

In the case of serious self-attack such as depression, guilt, or shame, our self-talk is unusually acrid and hateful. It can result in tremendous anxiety about our worth as an individual and as a human being. It can also result in high anxiety about the debilitated state that results from this kind of atrocious self-talk. We cannot feel like we are falling apart and losing the ability to function without feeling deeply anxious about the prospects of our survival. Here we are morally obligated to save our self from our self and move to a more compassionate mode of speaking to ourselves.

Thus far we have identified several methods for overcoming anxiety, most of which involve developing the self and working with our inner processes. Sometimes, however, there are more practical things that can be done to help anxiety. Many of these have been explored by Dale Carnegie in his book, *How to Stop Worrying and Start Living*. Some of them, in combination with thoughts of my own, are listed below. [3]

- Ask yourself what the worst thing is that could possibly happen if you cannot solve your problem. Prepare yourself to mentally accept the worst if necessary. Then calmly work to improve on the worst, which you have already accepted.*
- View each day as a sealed "day-tight" compartment. Do not get ahead of yourself. Focus on one day at a time.* Better yet, stay focused in the present moment.**

- Remember the terrible toll anxiety takes on the body. Ask yourself if losing your health is worth all this worry. Are you willing to die young?*
- Analyze your problems. Get the facts. Do not attempt to make a decision or formulate a game plan without the facts. Once you have them, carefully weigh them before you decide what to do.*
- When you decide what to do, go into action. Put your energies into implementing your plan without concern about the outcome.*
- When you find yourself becoming anxious, ask yourself these questions: What is the problem? What is the cause of the problem? What are all possible solutions? What are the best solutions?*
- Keep busy so there is less time to ruminate on worrisome things.*
- Do not focus on the small things in life. Keep annoying trifles in their place. Little things should not be allowed to ruin your happiness.*
- Use the law of averages. Ask yourself what the odds are that the worrisome event will even happen.*
- Accept and cooperate with the inevitable.* Acknowledge what you do not control.**
- Institute a stop-loss on your anxieties. Decide how much anxiety a given situation is worth and then refuse to give it anymore.*
- Do not try to resurrect what is already gone. "Do not try to saw sawdust."*
- Fill your mind with thoughts of health, hope, peace, and courage.* Thoughts precede physical reality.**
- Count your blessings, not your difficulties.* Start a gratitude list to help you stay focused on all that you do have.**

- Do not waste time trying to get even with your enemies.* It is draining, time-consuming, expensive, anxiety producing, and can be hurtful to you.**

- Do not expect gratitude from others, for it is not the norm.* Do not expect to be heard and understood either, for it happens rarely. This will reduce the amount of anxiety-producing anger that you carry.**

- Practice being yourself. Forget image, envy, and imitation.*

- Turn lemons into lemonade. Whenever possible, profit from your losses; turn your liabilities into assets.*

- Turn your depressive, anxious, inward-moving energy into outward-moving energy by doing something for others.** Take the focus off your own unhappiness and make someone else happy.*

- Call on your religious faith or spiritual philosophy if you have one.* Stop trying to understand why something happened. Stop trying to second-guess the universe. If you are spiritually oriented, consider the possibility that this is all part of a larger plan.**

- If you are worried about criticism, consider the fact that criticism is oftentimes based on envy or jealously. It is done to level the playing field or make another feel inferior. Others would not bother to criticize you if you were not a contender or a threat to them. Unjust criticism is a compliment of sorts.*

- Ignore unjust criticism if you know in your heart that you are right. Do not spend a lot of time trying to pacify or correct others. Get used to the idea that you will be criticized.*

- If you have anxiety about criticism, you can take stock of your own shortcomings or ask for honest, helpful, unbiased criticism from a trusted source. This helps you correct your areas of weakness before others even notice them.* This also takes the focus off being perfect and helps you move away from your idealized self.**

- Learn to laugh at yourself and at life's absurdities.**
- Rest before you get tired.* Take a break before your efficiency starts to wane. Eat a snack before your blood sugar bottoms out.**
- Learn to relax at home, work, or school.* Breathe. Relax your muscles. Rest your eyes. Meditate. Take a walk. Look out the window. Imagine a beautiful scene. Exercise. Repeat an affirmation.**
- Develop the following work habits. Clear your desk except for papers relating to what you are working on. Do things in order of their importance. Solve problems right away if you have the facts available to do so. Learn to supervise, deputize, and organize.* Ask for help if necessary. Delegate tasks whenever possible.**
- Finish projects so there are not too many things pulling on you from all directions. If you cannot finish some of them, take a few items off the list for a while.**
- To avoid worry and fatigue, be enthusiastic about your work.*
- Do not worry about insomnia.* Even if all you can do is quietly lie awake in bed, you will achieve a good deal of rest.** Insomnia does not kill you; worrying about it will harm you.*
- Have small realistic goals so that you can build success in your life. These can be in service of a larger, overall goal, but the larger goal must be tackled in increments.**
- Behave as though the whole world is watching everything you do and say so that you will not live in fear of being exposed or unmasked. Nor will you live in regret, guilt, or shame.**

- When times are tough, do not eschew work that is beneath your usual standards of employment. There is honor in work of any kind.**
- Live simply and within your means.**
- Do not accept a position that is far above your competency level. A challenge is one thing, but signing up for certain failure is another.**
- Before you do anything, ask yourself "Am I at peace with this?" If peace eludes you, do not do it.**
- Things do not happen *to you*. Things just happen. The message here is not to take things personally. Do not be concerned that something happened because you are being punished. This is not what is happening.**

*Dale Carnegie
**Stormy Smoleny Ph.D.

Chapter 21

TRIGGERS AND SELF-ATTACK

There is one last technique to be discussed that can be very helpful with stemming the tide of self-attack. This is the technique of working with our triggers. Whereas triggers are not directly related to self-attack, they are being discussed here because they oftentimes activate preexisting areas of self-attack such as guilt, shame, self-recrimination, and depression. Our triggers do this swiftly, leaving little opportunity for observation, reflection, or resolution. Once we are affected by a trigger, all we know is that we are instantly back in pain from the reemergence of something unpleasant from our past. Sometimes we do not even know that this is a repeat performance. We are completely unaware that our heightened emotional state is connected to a past event. We simply feel upset, angry, depressed, or irritable. We are also usually highly reactive to anything that occurs in our environment. However, if we are aware of the presence of a trigger, see it for what it is, and notice its impact, we can step back, detach, and keep our wits about us rather than fall helplessly into a self-attacking replay of an objectionable event.

A trigger is a stimulus that provokes a strong reaction within us. It can be an event, a word or phrase, a facial expression, a specific demeanor or mannerism, a certain way of behaving, a tone of voice, a level of attentiveness or lack of it, or a level of respect or lack of it, to name a few kinds of triggers. It is typically an external catalyst that sets off or activates something that is already present internally. As such, it is not the primary cause of our reaction, but more of an activator of something that is already present. Usually it is the stimulator of an unresolved issue or an unpleasant memory. It can also serve to highlight and stimulate an undesirable personality trait (predictable behavior/response pattern) that we do not wish to acknowledge.

A life experience that triggers an unresolved issue, unpleasant memory, or undesirable personality trait is quite different from a life experience that would elicit a strong emotional reaction in almost anyone. This is important to understand, as we are not to berate ourselves for having a strong, healthy emotional response to someone who is treating us poorly and/or inflicting pain. To be clear, when we speak of triggers, we are talking about activators of preexisting areas of pain, conflict, or behavioral response.

There are also internal triggers that exist due to biological processes such as hunger, hormonal imbalances, disease, imbalanced brain chemistry, or sexual need. These can cause emotional responses by themselves. However, like external triggers, they can also activate areas of inner turmoil that predate the current biological trigger.

When any of these preexisting parts of us are stimulated, we usually experience higher levels of negative emotion. We may feel angry, critical, afraid, hurt, guilty, ashamed, misunderstood, or rejected. Our behavior may become reactive and not nearly as controlled as usual. In general, when triggered, we do not exhibit the level of emotional or behavioral control that we normally do.

For instance, perhaps someone has said something about our level of responsibility not being what it should be regarding a minor oversight. They have arrogantly stalked away, leaving us powerless to respond. Our reaction to this is intensely negative. We know that we are highly responsible and that the incident at hand is not at all indicative of how we generally function. Usually we are stellar performers who exhibit a great deal of responsibility. The incident reminds us of memories from our past when we sincerely tried to do our best, but still were criticized, berated, and misunderstood. It also reminds us of times when there were unrealistic demands for perfection placed upon us. We are enraged that we keep trying so hard only to be misunderstood once again. We are sick of people who cannot begin to see us as we are. We are also exhausted and disgusted that perfection seems to be the only acceptable standard for success. We get very aggressive, say things to those around us that we wish we had not, and stomp out the door. We then turn things against ourselves for not speaking up, pronounce ourselves to be worthless, and go eat a pint of ice cream. We are emotionally and behaviorally out of control.

We could have used this triggering incident to acknowledge the terrible pain our emotional self has endured so many times in the past when others could not see, acknowledge, or appreciate its heartfelt efforts. We could have apologized to our emotional self for not having seen its pain before this. We could have strongly defended it and assured it that it did not have to be perfect. But we did not. We got reactive, lashed out at others, lashed out at our self, and behaved poorly all the way around.

As illustrated in this example, when we are triggered and experiencing a heightened level of reactivity, we can either turn our negative feelings toward others or toward ourselves. Both involve an upset emotional self; the blaming, attacking messages are just directed differently.

Most of the time, we do not even realize that our blaming and attacking behaviors are fueled by our activated issues. We are too busy judging the person or situation that served as a trigger or we are lost in our own self-recriminations. Certainly we are not in the mood to identify our unresolved issues, painful memories, or unwanted personality traits. Nor are we predisposed to determine what our messaging is to our emotional self.

Luckily, once we calm down, we can use our triggers to gain an awareness of what our emotional issues are and/or what disowned aspects of ourselves we so dislike. We begin to see that our present-day reactions to life's triggers are linked to specific areas of pain from our past. Alternatively, we begin to notice that the undesirable traits we most react to in others reflect similar ones within our self. In other words, we can turn outward reactivity into inward looking.

Turning outward reactivity into inward looking is a wonderful way to short-circuit self-attack. It is also a great way to reclaim any judged or disowned parts of our self. Most importantly, our inner looking can help us gain an awareness of our emotional self's needs. Any time we notice that we have been triggered, we should quickly and automatically ask ourselves "What part of me needs comfort, acceptance, and support? What part of me is presenting itself for healing?"

When we have determined what hateful things we have been saying to our self, we need to immediately apologize to the emotional self. We need to say "I love you. I'm sorry. Please forgive me. Thank you."[1] We must make this a practice that is done as often as necessary. Keep apologizing. Be sincere. Your pain will stop.

If we cannot determine exactly how we are attacking ourselves and therefore do not know what to apologize for, we can at least apologize to the emotional self for having to put up with whatever is externally occurring. In this way, we can continue to validate the emotional self as a valued and cared-for part of self. We can let it know that we wish we could protect it from all of life's slings and arrows even when we cannot. At least we can let it know that it is not alone and that half of the things it has to endure are ridiculous to begin with.

What we are trying to do with all this attention to the emotional self is threefold.

- First, we are trying to provide a good holding environment for what it has to say. That means that when it expresses its feelings, we are there to hear them, to catch them, and to contain them. In doing so, we have not let these feelings be flung out into darkness without a soul to care about them. We have brought them into the realm of our awareness and we have given them value.

- Second, in apologizing to the emotional self, we are bringing it succor. We are recognizing its plight and comforting it in every way we can. We are offering support, assistance, and relief from pain.
- Third, by apologizing to our emotional self for having hidden or judged any part of it, we reclaim our formerly disowned parts of self and help ourselves become less fragmented and more whole.

However, it is not just the emotional self that deserves an apology. The individuals acting as triggers need an apology as well. As strange as this sounds, it is an important component in our efforts to mitigate the effects of a trigger. We may need to mentally apologize for judging the triggering persons, for our unwillingness to understand their position or their pain, for confusing their actions with our own issues from the past, or for being impatient and abrasive in our interactions with them. We need to apologize for whatever we can think of. If we cannot think of anything to apologize for, we can simply offer a general apology, or apologize for not being ready to apologize.

Another thing we can do is attempt to see others' pains and problems within ourselves and then work to heal those issues through forgiveness of the self. This allows us to get a better sense of other people's struggles as well as our own. It softens our outlook and fosters a sense of oneness. It is healing for both parties.

Here is one more possibility. This will sound even stranger than the last, but it works. We can apologize to a triggering dog, a cat, or any other living thing. We can even mentally apologize to what we would normally deem inanimate objects that may be involved in a triggering situation. We can apologize to anything at all. The main thing is that the quality of our energy changes from an aggressive, judgmental, hard-hitting one to a smoother, milder, peaceful one. Our serenity moves us away from blame and redirects us to humble inward looking. Once we have done the above, our life events will have little power to trigger us. They will only be occurrences that help us to know ourselves and heal ourselves.

In a way, our triggers and the emotional self's reactions to them, provide a great service to us. Without the two, we would be hard pressed to know what is going on inside of us. Of course, we are already aware of some of what is going on within us, but since most of the content of our inner world resides in the unconscious, it is almost impossible to access unless something brings it to light. Our triggers and the emotional responses they garner do just that. They show us something that we probably did not know was present; they show us something that needs to be resolved or cleared. As such, they provide a great opportunity.

Because our triggers and our emotional responses to them have provided us with such an exceptional opportunity for growth, we need to not only internally apologize to anyone or anything who serves as a trigger, but thank them as well. We also need to thank our emotional self for bringing us the eye-opening experience that it has brought us.

None of the above suggestions are meant to force us to prematurely forgive someone. This would be abusive to an already injured emotional self. We are not looking for a grudging mutual handshake while still raging inside. Apologizing and asking another for forgiveness is just a first inner step toward peace of mind. The person receiving our apology never even has to know we have done so, but on an energetic level something will begin to shift, something will start to improve.

While we are not responsible for the actions of others, we are responsible for using our triggers and the responses they bring forward to clear ourselves of self-judgment and self-hatred. Of course, we do not have to accept this responsibility, but if we choose to do so, it will not only help bring serenity to our self and others, but will also reduce or terminate further reactivity.

When we are able to work with our triggers constructively, we are able to detach from whatever occurs in life. We only stay attached because of our own unresolved issues, disparaging evaluations of others, and critical self-judgments, which keep us reacting to whatever life brings. They keep us tied tight and reacting over and over. Since we cannot control what life brings, we can at least detach and try to usher in peace.

Chapter 22

FINAL THOUGHTS

Throughout this book we have explored many specific ways to work with our emotions. All are valuable in their own right and can lead us to emotional balance. Yet there is one remaining overall concept that we have not explored sufficiently which can also lead to emotional balance. That is the concept of acceptance.

To accept in the conventional sense simply means that we agree to take something that is offered. This implies choice. In a philosophical sense, *to accept* means that we agree to receive whatever life brings us with acquiescence and grace. This does not imply choice regarding what we are receiving; however, it does allow us the choice to embrace a compliant attitude over a resistant one. When we choose to comply rather than resist, we give that which we are accepting a favorable reception. It is possible that we may not have wanted or chosen whatever it is that we receive, yet we give it a place in our lives. We give it space, we give it the right to be there, and when needed we give it our careful attention.

In our quest for emotional balance, we always need to remain mindful of how we are or are not accepting what has been given to us. This is especially true when whatever we have received would not necessarily have been our choice. If we think that our life circumstances are due to our own choices and behaviors, we can take responsibility for them, ruefully grin and bear them, and hopefully make a course correction. However, when we are up against something that we think has not been created by us, the circumstances are much harder to accept. We feel trapped, betrayed, resentful, hopeless, and angry. This drains our energy, makes us bitter, and robs us of our emotional balance.

The resistance mode is incredibly strenuous; in fact, it is exhausting. We rage at injustice, punch at shadows, and scream into the darkness until we are spent. Yet even if what we are called upon to accept is extremely difficult, when we agree to stop judging what is in front of us, our straining and striving stops. All the energy that we had been using to fight our circumstances is now freed to help us solve problems about our new circumstances.

Despite this viable way out of our emotional churning, we are judging and resisting much of the time and fighting against what we have been handed or what we have created in our lives. It is rather reflexive. The emotional self finds itself in pain and so we reject the circumstances surrounding that pain. In these instances we can use all the tools given in this book to make ourselves feel better. This includes accepting "what is." If we add this element to our lives, our emotional processing will go much faster and better for us. The key is consenting to the presence of whatever is upsetting us rather than disowning it.

When we refuse to accept whatever is happening, we are saying that we object to the feelings surrounding it. We may be saying that we object to feeling our pain, that we object to accepting life's limitations, or that we object to seeing ourselves realistically. We may be objecting to a painful loss, to an enforced change of plans, to the actions and limitations of another person, or to shattered dreams. There is so much that we resist.

Yet when we resist life, we are usually stuck with our pain. We cannot process our feelings effectively nor get on with finding new pathways and making new choices. We are pretty much stuck hating life.

When we accept with grace, however, an amazing change takes place. We can process our feelings more effectively and we can look reality in the face. We can stop long enough to see what our new circumstances look like, feel like, and are like. Even if we dislike what we have been called upon to accept, we can say to ourselves, "Let me see what being sad, lonely, limited, or disappointed is like." In fact, we could agree to experience it all in detail. If we did, we would most likely see that it is all pretty interesting and that there is a tremendous release in experiencing rather than resisting.

Here is an example of how we may speak to ourselves when choosing acceptance. "So I'm in financial straits for a while. Let me see what being poor is like. Let me see what I can do to live simply while in this phase of my life. Let me take a look at what I can do to fulfill myself emotionally while in this circumstance. Let me see what I can do to take the pressure off of myself now and eventually build in a new direction. I can be in this circumstance now without identifying with victim consciousness. I don't control any of this right now, so I'll just do what I can and trust that the tide will turn. I know that everything is cyclical and that this will eventually pass. This isn't going to kill me."

It should be noted that acceptance of reality does not mean that we are to sit back and do nothing. We may simply need to do different activities than we normally do. We may need to work harder than we usually do. Conversely, we may need to engage in less stressful activities and rest more. We may have to spend less to accommodate a budget or spend more if we need legal counsel. We may need to work at a new type of job. We may have to take on a different role. We may have to ask for help. We may even be dependent on others for a while. There are many ways we can accommodate our circumstances. We must simply work within the realm of reality. While we are doing so, we can work to better our current reality and devise strategies for moving our lives forward into a more prosperous cycle. Soon enough the current downward cycle will be over and a less arduous one will commence.

Accepting whatever life brings is tied to living in the present moment. The present moment is our only point of reality. It is the only place where we can function in a meaningful way. In the present moment, the past is no longer in existence and the future is merely a plethora of possibilities. If we wish not to be hampered by our past and to bring forth a chosen possibility from our future, we need to act effectively in the here and now. In each consecutive new moment we must build on our chosen possibility until we have turned it into reality.

If we have accepted a challenging cycle for what it is (a time of decrease or difficulty) and have agreed to gracefully live within its bounds for a while, we have essentially agreed with ourselves to live within the present moment. We are not railing about the past or idly dreaming about a nebulous future. We are meeting the challenges of our present reality moment by moment and are not getting too far ahead of ourselves. We may be working on developing a future possibility that we wish to bring forward at some point, but that is being done by using each present moment effectively.

It should be noted that we cannot effectively use each present moment if we are anesthetizing ourselves with substances such as alcohol or illicit drugs. While we may sometimes find the need for controlled, monitored medical help when in a downward cycle, ongoing numbing of the self with uncontrolled substances is a complete waste of our present moment and our creative capacity.

Of course, it goes without saying that acceptance does not mean the choice to sustain abuse. In cases of abuse, acceptance may be letting in the realization that our current setting is not the place in which we are going to stay. Here we will be using each present moment to plan for a move to a safer and more life-affirming environment. We must never confuse acceptance with a willingness to place ourselves in harm's way.

Acceptance of our present reality is also tied to our capacity for humility. None of us know why things play out the way they do. None of us understand the workings of the universe. We can only conjecture about the purpose, meaning, or learning opportunity that each cycle provides. So when we hear ourselves judging whatever the universe brings forth, we need to step back and lay down our hubris. We need to entertain the possibility that there may be a purpose to our present reality far beyond our ability to comprehend.

The tools given in this book can only be implemented within the present moment. We can only observe ourselves, know ourselves, work with ourselves, forgive ourselves, and speak kindly to ourselves in each present moment that we have consented to experience. A lot rides on what we choose to do in this regard. We must always remember that our peace of mind and our creative power is in accepting each successive present moment and then deciding what to do with each of those moments. Anyone can do it. Why not start today?

Endnotes

Chapter 6
1. https//psychcentral.com/15 Common Cognitive Distortions.
2. Campbell, *Psychiatric Dictionary* (p. 526).
3. Ibid., (p. 526).
4. Viorst, *Necessary Losses* (pp. 161-169).
5. Campbell, *Psychiatric Dictionary* (p. 526).

Chapter 7
1. Beckwith, *Life Visioning Workbook* (p. 16).
2. YouTube.com. *70's Mother Nature *Chiffon* Margarine Commercial.*™

Chapter 8
1. McWilliams, *Psychoanalytic Diagnosis* (pp. 96-144).
2. Campbell, *Psychiatric Dictionary* (p. 213).

Chapter 12
1. DeRohan, *Right Use of Will* (p. 18).
2. Ibid., (p. 18).
3. Ibid., (p. 18).

Chapter 15
1. Rubin, *Compassion and Self-Hate.*
2. Spotnitz, *Psychotherapy of Preoedipal Conditions* (p. 104).

Chapter 16
1. Rubin, *Compassion and Self-Hate* (pp. 69-73).

2. Horney, *Neurosis and Human Growth: The Struggle Toward Self-Realization.*

Chapter 17
1. Rubin, *Compassion and Self-Hate* (pp. 74-80).
2. Ibid., (pp. 90-91).
3. Ibid., (pp. 91-92).
4. Ibid., (pp. 93-94).
5. Ibid., (pp. 93-94).
6. Ibid., (pp. 91-92).
7. Ibid., (p. 152).
8. Ibid., (pp. 106-110).
9. Ibid., (p. 153).
10. Ibid., (pp. 157-158).
11. Ibid., (p. 149).
12. Ibid., (pp. 150-151).

Chapter 18
1. www.goodreads.com/author/quotes/3503.Maya_Angelou.

Chapter 19
1. Peck, *The Road Less Traveled* (p. 1).
2. Viewonbuddhism.org/4_noble_truths.html.

Chapter 20
1. Campbell, *Psychiatric Dictionary* (pp. 48-49).
2. Ibid., (p. 48).
3. Carnegie, *How to Stop Worrying and Start Living* (pp. 36, 54, 109, 186, 189-209, 228, 271).

Chapter 21
1. Youtube/Dr. Hew Len 1 0f 9 ho'oponopono.

Bibliography

Angelou, Maya. *Maya Angelou Quotes*. Retrieved on February 10, 2017 from www.goodreads.com/author/quotes/3503 Maya Angelou.

Beckwith, Michael Bernard. (2008). *Life Visioning Workbook*. Boulder CO: Sounds True, Inc.

Campbell, Robert J. (1989). *Psychiatric Dictionary*. New York, NY: Oxford University Press.

Carnegie, Dale. (1984). *How to Stop Worrying and Start Living: Time-Tested Methods For Conquering Worry*. New York, NY: Simon and Schuster.

Casarjian, Robin. (1992). *Forgiveness: A Bold Choice for a Peaceful Heart*: New York, NY: Bantam Books.

Crakkerjakk. (2007). *70's Mother Nature *Chiffon* Margarine Commercial*.™ Retrieved on February 10, 2017 from www.youtube.com/watch?v=LLrTPrp-fW8.

DeRohan, Ceanne. (1984). *Right Use of Will: Healing and Evolving the Emotional Body*. Santa Fe, NM: Four Winds Publications.

Grohol, J. (2016). *15 Common Cognitive Distortions*. Retrieved on February 10, 2017 from https//psychcentral.com.

Harderwijk, Rudy. (2016). *A View on Buddhism: The Four Noble Truths*. Retrieved on February 10, 2017 from www.viewonbuddhism.org/4_noble_truths.html.

Hew Len. (2009). *1 of 9 Ho'oponopono*. Retrieved on February 10, 2017 from www.youtube.com.1of9Ho'oponopono.

Horney, Karen. (1991). *Neurosis and Human Growth: The Struggle Toward Self-Realization*. New York, NY: W.W. Norton and Company.

McWilliams, Nancy. (1994). *Psychoanalytic Diagnosis: Understanding Personality Structure in the Clinical Process.* New York, NY: Guilford Press.

Melemis, Steven. *A Guide to Cognitive Therapy.* Retrieved on February 10, 2017 from www.Cognitivetherapyguide.org.

Peck, M. Scott. (1978). *The Road Less Traveled: A New Psychology of Love, Traditional Values and Spiritual Growth.* New York, NY: Simon and Schuster.

Rubin, Theodore Isaac. (1975). *Compassion and Self-Hate: An Alternative to Despair.* New York, NY: Ballantine Books.

Spotnitz, H. (1976). *Psychotherapy of Preoedipal Conditions: Schizophrenia and Severe Character Disorders.* New York, NY: Jason Aronson, Inc.

Viorst, Judith. (1986). *Necessary Losses: The Loves, Illusions, Dependencies and Impossible Expectations That All of Us Have to Give Up in Order to Grow.* New York NY: Ballantine Books.

About the Author

Stormy Smoleny, Ph.D., LMHC, NCPsyA, LP is a licensed mental health counselor in the state of Florida (MH1448), a licensed psychoanalyst in New York state (000595-1), and a nationally certified psychoanalyst (P931223). She has post-doctoral certification in psychoanalysis, a doctorate in counseling psychology, and a master's degree in management/organizational psychology. At the time of this printing, she has been in private practice for thirty-six years, and has worked with individuals, couples, families, and groups. Before going into clinical practice, she worked as an organizational psychologist assisting organizations with teambuilding, stress management, and conflict resolution. She has taught psychology courses at Miami-Dade College for over thirty years.

Dr. Smoleny's preferred method of treatment is psychoanalysis, which is defined as the observation, description, evaluation, and interpretation of dynamic unconscious mental processes that contribute to the formation of personality and behavior. Her goal is to identify and resolve unconscious psychic problems that affect interpersonal relationships and emotional development, to facilitate changes in personality and behavior, and to develop adaptive functioning.

Dr. Smoleny's specialty is modern psychoanalysis. This is an orientation that offers a corrective emotional experience rather than intellectual interpretations and explanations. The term *corrective emotional experience* means that the patient is healed through emotional communication and interaction with the analyst. Within an emotionally corrective setting there is opportunity for the release of negative emotion, for emotional needs to be met, and for awareness to evolve naturally. It is an environment that fosters maturation and development through a present-moment healing experience.

Dr. Smoleny has also studied philosophy, spirituality, metaphysics, nutrition, exercise, and alternative healing. For those who prefer a more holistic approach to psychotherapy, she offers a unique blend of traditional and non-traditional thought.

Dr. Smoleny lives in Miami, Florida with her husband of 50 years. She has two children and four grandchildren who live nearby. She hopes to write a book for each grandchild. Dr. Smoleny has also written *In Search of the Unwanted Self* and *Truths from the Self: Insights into Finding Wisdom in the Present Moment*, available on Amazon.com and Bookmasters.com.